Mountain Bikes

by the editors of *Bicycling*® magazine

Rodale Press, Emmaus, Pennsylvania

Printed in the United States of America on recycled paper containing a high percentage of de-inked fiber.

Edited by Susan Weaver
Illustrations by Wally Niebart

Library of Congress Cataloging-in-Publication Data

Mountain bikes.

    1. All terrain cycling – United States. 2. All terrain bicycles.
I. Bicycling!
GV1043.7.M68   1988   796.6'0973   88-3135
ISBN 0-87857-755-6 (pbk. : alk. paper)

2 4 6 8 10 9 7 5 3   paperback

Contents

Introduction 1

**Part One: The Wild and Wonderful World
of Mountain Bikes** 3

Hit the Dirt – Off-Road Riding Can Make You
a Better Cyclist 4

More Grace than Gonz – Observed Trials Riding . . . 7

Fat-Tire Racing – Don't It Make You Want
to Shout 'Mama!' 12

Roadies and Mudders Go Head-to-Head
over Fitness 19

Part Two: Equipment to Suit Every Taste and Budget . . . 25

The ABCs of Buying an ATB 26

The Bikes Have Never Been Better 32

Time to Re-Tire? 39

The Right Stuff for Off-Road 44

Dirty Duds – All-Terrain Clothing Comes of Age . . . 52

Maintaining Your Machine – What to Do
so the Dirt Won't Hurt 54

Part Three: Off-Road Riding Skills and Street Smarts . . . 59

Get Good – Then You Can Get Gonzo 60

The Mountain Comes to You – Develop Trail Skills
at Home 65

Mastering the Ups and Downs 67
Putting Yourself on Trials 70
Advanced Off-Road Drills 74
Taking Your Knobbies to Town . . . Safely 76
Let It Snow – With Fat Tires You Can Thumb
   Your Nose at Winter 79

Part Four: Scenic Trails and Backroad Routes **83**
Mountain Biking the Backcountry –
   Six Terrific Areas 84
Off-Road Vacations the Easy Way –
   Organized Group Tours 88

Credits **91**

Introduction

They're adult toys. They're practical transportation. They're escape vehicles, outdoor exercycles, serious racing machines. They may take you touring in the wilds, commuting in your urban jungle, or simply riding down your own street. They're the bike of a thousand faces . . .

And a dozen names. These bicycles, whose cushy wide tires and strong rims can ride over or through almost anything, whose low, low gearing can practically scale walls, and whose upright or flat handlebars let you feel comfortable doing it, are variously known: Mountain bike. All-terrain bike, or ATB. Fat-tire bike. Off-road bike. Clunker. Ballooner. Bomber. Flyer. And with some modifications, city bike. No one name seems to capture the essence of the machine, but that's okay.

The machine continues to capture the interest of cyclists everywhere. From wild, wacky, to-the-limit trail riders to merely mortal comfort-seekers who may never take it off the pavement. And lots of folks in between.

So it's no surprise you're interested. Through the mountain bike you've found a whole new way of cycling. You own a ballooner/bomber/ATB, or you're about to. By the way, if you're shopping now, you'll make a well-informed purchase by first reading the consumer guide section in this book.

In these pages you'll also discover a host of new ways to enjoy mountain biking and just as many techniques to make you a more skilled, confident, (and why not?) flashier rider. So dig in. Even if you intend the quietest of off-road pursuits, in this book

1

you'll find ways to enhance the experience. And when vacation time rolls around, if you find you don't want to leave your mountain bike at home, check into an ATB tour from our list or plan your own trip with our leads to some of the best country for riding in the United States. Either way, you'll find a great way to travel.

This book can be just as invaluable as your knobbies in exploring the world of mountain biking and developing your potential to make the most of it.

Part One
The Wild and Wonderful World of Mountain Bikes

Hit the Dirt-Off-Road Riding
Can Make You a Better Cyclist

When the first mountain bikes appeared, their riders were often stereotyped as unwashed gonzos who disengaged their brains before bombing downhill. Meanwhile, this fraternity of mudders considered traditional road riders, resplendent in their skin-tight, color-coordinated nylon/Lycra, a bunch of too-serious snobs.

But times have changed. More and more cyclists are realizing that a bike's a bike, and they're riding both all-terrain bikes and road machines for fun and fitness. One cyclist who finds the two sports not only compatible but also complementary is Ned Overend, the 1986 National Off-Road champion. After spending most of that season on the dirt he qualified for the U.S. National Amateur Road team and competed in the World Championships – strong evidence that off-road skills can contribute to on-road performance.

If you're a road rider contemplating buying an ATB, hesitate no longer. It's one of the best ways to improve overall riding ability.

Take bike-handling. No matter how skilled you are at keeping the rubber on the pavement, there'll always be challenges, whether it's lousy drivers, snarling dogs, or slippery corners. Riding an ATB on dirt, snow, or grass is the best and safest way to improve balance and control. As Overend observes, "On an ATB you get used to losing traction, so when that happens on the road, you don't panic."

Some off-road riders develop uncanny bike-handling abilities. Tom Hayles, a Colorado cyclocross champ, says, "I've been in road races where I was able to get away just because I could slide through wet, downhill corners while everyone else was slowing down."

Surprisingly, such wizardry doesn't require much formal practice. You'll learn many of these skills by just following off-road trails. As champion road racer Rebecca Twigg Whitehead explains, "At the Olympic training camp our dirt rides are basically free-form. There are a lot of little roads where we chase each other around." Even if terrain in your area isn't too demanding, simply increasing your speed will make an easy trail tougher.

If you prefer a more formal practice course, devise a half-mile loop in a park or field that includes six or eight corners (some at the bottom of hills to increase difficulty). Route the course around trees or rocks, through mudholes, and over footbridges or logs. Then ride it fast enough to slalom past obstacles, slide through slippery spots, and skid around corners.

Think you're getting good? Invite some friends for a dirt

Photograph 1-1. Want a great way to have fun, vary your riding, and improve bike-handling? Go off-road with a mountain bike.

criterium. Don't forget to wear helmets and protective clothing, including knee and elbow pads if you're really getting into it. After off-road action like this, even the tightest paceline or peloton won't seem so frightening.

Muscle Makers

Mountain biking builds leg strength, too. Near his home in Durango, Colorado, Overend routinely climbs hills so steep it's hard to maintain traction. "This really helps develop my power," he says. Even riding regularly through mud, snow, and grass can make you a feared crank cracker.

Riding off-road also strengthens your upper body as you pull on the handlebars to conquer hills and surmount obstacles. "You build muscles in your arms and shoulders that you wouldn't road riding," says Overend. "I think these muscles help your road riding."

To derive these extra benefits and avoid injury, it's important to maintain proper riding position. Your pedaling efficiency will increase and the chance of developing knee problems will be minimized if you approximate the same saddle position on your ATB as on your road bike. Small variations are permissible, however. For instance, Overend likes his ATB saddle farther back because he doesn't wear cleats. This lets him push down on the pedals with maximum force. Dave Meyer, another Colorado cyclist who finished eighth in the Off-Road Nationals, positions his ATB saddle slightly forward to ease stress on his back muscles during climbs.

Although you'll have to experiment to find your ideal saddle position, it's a cardinal rule not to overgear. Plodding up hills at 40 rpm will keep you from developing valuable power, and will eventually destroy your knees. As with a road bike, choose low enough gears for your ATB to let you spin over tough spots. Even strong riders in the mountain bike mecca of Crested Butte, Colorado, pack a granny chainring of 26 or 24 teeth.

Be sure to mix your ATB and road riding wisely, however. Meyer, a Category II road racer, says he used to be "a criterium specialist but now in those flat, fast ones I don't have the speed and snap I used to." Overend recommends, "Mix up your training and work on your road spin. You certainly can't train for the road solely on an ATB."

Perhaps the greatest advantage to off-road riding is the variety it offers. On an ATB, the number of possible training routes is infinite. Dirt and gravel roads, canal banks, city parks, jogging trails – they're all open for exploration. When you become a bit jaded after 6 days of road work, refresh yourself with a roll in the dirt. You may even make new friends riding off-road, though some might caution against bringing them home.

One common misconception about off-road riding has to do with safety. If you wear proper gear and take the necessary precautions, cycling off-road is actually much less dangerous than pedaling along a city street. There are no cars, no trucks, and should you crash, the landing is much softer.

And if the spirit is willing but the wallet is weak, consider that the quality of ATBs has never been better. Technology is such that you can buy a durable mountain bike with a strong frame, sealed bearings, and bombproof tires for between $350 and $500. The wear you'll save on your road bike may be worth that much. Plus, on days when the weather is miserable, you'll have a trusty backup to battle the elements.

More Grace than Gonz – Observed Trials Riding

It's a distant cousin to tightrope walking, a half-sister to ballet, and it bears a striking resemblance to golf, of all things. In actual lineage, however, it is the illegitimate son of that dirty, irreverent, pleasure monger known as fat-tire mountain biking.

We're talking about observed trials riding, an up-and-coming cycle sport that demands more grace than gonz. You don't have to get grimy to do it well. You would benefit from the balance of Baryshnikov, the concentration of Nicklaus, but you don't need the physique of a Schwarzenegger. Success depends as much on mind over matter as it does on your muscles.

Although it has been pursued only recently in this country, trials riding has developed a devoted following. In September 1985 at Wendell State Forest in northern Massachusetts, more than 300 mountain bikers from across the country gathered for Ross Bicycles' Fat Tire 3-Day Stage Race, which featured trials riding as one of the events. What transpired was entertaining, even humorous as the best off-road riders in the country suppressed their manic desires to go fast and for one day concentrated on tiptoeing their way through Smokey the Bear country.

To appreciate the challenge of trials riding, it's necessary to understand its nuances. A natural, picturesque setting is preferred, whether it be the woodsy, maple-syrup-and-pine-cone surroundings of New England or the sunny, surf-side environs of southern California. But if you're not so environmentally blessed, you can still make do.

A trials course normally consists of a number of sections, similar to holes on a golf course. They can be of varying lengths and levels of difficulty, but each should test a rider's bike-handling skills. One section, for example, might snake through a mine field of rocks and fallen trees. Another might plunge into a mud hole or sand pit before climbing a hill. One more may incorporate railroad ties, 55-gallon drums, or even a junked automobile.

Competitors are not permitted to ride a section before the event, but they are encouraged to investigate. The experts will walk it many times, eyes to the ground and hands on their hips, searching for the path of least resistance. Some actually envision themselves aboard their bicycles, front tires rolling here and back tires skidding there. Others take a more casual approach, openly discussing strategy with teammates, competitors, and even spectators.

Eventually, the judge's cry of "Rider up!" clears the course. The crowd grows silent. A challenger's eyes narrow with concentration, then he or she proceeds to pick and power his or her way through the obstacle course. The audience quietly oohs and aahs at each nimble move and then breaks into a smattering of appreciative applause at the finish.

As with golf, the lowest score wins. In trials riding, 0 is the best a rider can do, meaning he or she was able to complete the section without *dabbing,* touching a foot to the ground. At the other end of the scale, a 5 means failure. A fall, a flattened course marker, a missed gate, or putting both feet down simultaneously earns you that. In between, single points (to a maximum of 3 per section) are awarded for each dab. Elapsed time is of no importance and scoring is done on a cumulative, section-by-section basis.

Although many of us probably played similar games as children, carving our own makeshift courses out of vacant lots and overgrown fields, trials riding is not as easy as it may sound. Often, the twitter of wood sparrows or the shiver of windblown palms is interrupted by a healthy cussword. More than one frustrated rider has even been known to pitch his or her bike into the drink as if it were a traitorous nine iron.

The Class of the Competition

He came from Newport Beach, California, an unlikely home for the master of a predominantly East Coast event. Unlike the majority of mountain bikers who had spent the weekend camping in Wendell State Forest and hence had the complexion of tree bark, he looked as if he had just emerged from a Beverly Hills salon. Hair, neatly cropped; face, clean-shaven and tan; teeth, as white as ocean spray.

While many of his competitors wore costumes of corduroy, flannel, and faded cotton, his was a spotless white-and-purple uniform crowned by a pink helmet. His matching bike, a custom Kuwahara with 24-inch wheels, was a similar work of art. Let the other riders treat their machines as if they were panzer tanks. His always rested carefully against a tree. It was rarely even dirty.

Because the Ross Stage Race was only his second major trials competition, few even knew his name. As a result, people referred to him with anonymous reverence as in "Which way did *he* go?"

Indeed, he was a wizard in the woods. In the morning's preliminary session, he completed all seven sections twice without so much as a single dab (his closest rival amassed 15 points). He could bring his bike to a complete stop, balancing interminably while he studied the path ahead. He could "bunny hop" around obstacles, jumping his bike as if it were a two-wheeled pogo stick. He could do wheelies on either tire. He could ride over picnic tables and cars. He was half stunt man, half strategist. He was 24-year-old Kevin Norton.

Photograph 1-2. The key to successful trials riding, says Norton, is control, whether you're picking your way through a rocky ditch or diving into the mouth of a hungry crater.

"I hope to show people that you don't have to go 100 mph to have fun," said Norton, who swept through the afternoon finals (seven more sections done five times apiece) to win the event by a 58-point margin (41 to 99). "Many of the big guys who ride hundreds of miles a week can't do this. Sure, it might not be as exciting to go slow, but it's harder and requires more balance. It takes more brains than muscle."

Actually, Norton got his start as a motorcycle trials rider, a career in which he excelled for 9 years. Originally, he adopted bicycling only to help him perfect his balance. Later he decided he liked this type of trialing best. Not only was it safer and more fun but, as a burgeoning sport, it offered him the chance to quickly become the best in the country. That was 1984. Soon after, he received a sponsorship from Kuwahara, SunTour, IRC, Rads, Everything Bicycles in Compton, California, and the Rainbow Bicycle Shop in Laguna Beach. In 1985, he proved his worth by winning the Trials Riding National Championship in Virginia City, Nevada.

To stay sharp, the 5-foot-9, 135-pound Norton surfs, runs, and rides his bicycle over every obstacle in his path. "You don't need a whole lot of athletic ability," he explains, "but it takes a lot of practice."

The Next Comeuppance

Although many of the mountain men in Wendell State Forest were frustrated by the trials, Norton demonstrated what good trials riding is and convinced more than one person of its potential. For instance, Joe Murray might have dominated the 3-day stage race even more than he did had he not struggled in the trials, amassing 42 points in the preliminaries and failing to make the finals.

According to race organizer and Ross public relations director John Kirkpatrick, many fat tire promoters have hesitated to include trials riding in stage races but are now beginning to realize its benefits. Not only can trials teach riders valuable bike-handling skills, but it's also a crowd pleaser. Unlike conventional races that offer spectators a fleeting glimpse of the action, observed trials let them hold their breath with every agonizing pedal stroke.

"No doubt about it, trials are the next comeuppance," said Jacquie Phelan, the women's general classification winner despite failing to make the trials finals. "You almost have to meditate to do it right. You also have to let go of your ego somewhat.

"Personally, I think trials are great. They allow the girls to catch up with the guys; even the spare-tire crowd now has the opportunity to beat the lean-and-mean crowd. You don't even have to maintain a 12-month fitness program to do it, although it would make a great indoor sport for the winter. Imagine riding over couches."

Fat-Tire Racing – Don't It Make You Want to Shout 'Mama!'

by Stuart Stevens

It was while I was flying over my handlebars in a long, slow-motion flip that it occurred to me I might still have a thing or two to learn about off-road racing. Since I spent what seemed at least half an hour en route from bicycle seat to terra firma, I had plenty of time for reflection.

"Gee," I thought just before the first bike began to run over me, "and I figured I was doing really well."

Truth was, I was less than a mile into a 40-mile race that was the centerpiece of the Chequamegon Fat Tire Festival. But hey, those first few hundred yards had gone just great. As I picked myself up, examining the perfect impression of a Ritchey Quad 1.9 tire tread running across my forearm, I found myself overwhelmed by a mad urge to giggle. So what if there were 39 more hilly miles and I was already beginning to look like I'd gone one-on-one with Rambo? This was serious, big-time FUN! Which was exactly what I'd traveled to the backwoods of Telemark, Wisconsin, to find.

Most people would consider a place like Telemark, or nearby Hayward, as legitimate contenders for the designation of "remote." As in the middle of nowhere. After all, it's more than 3 hours by car to Duluth, and Canada is lurking just across Lake Superior. This is real North Woods territory, home of the National Lumberjack Championships where descendants of the original Scandinavian settlers battle for honor with cross saws and axes.

But to a surprisingly large number of people, Telemark is as well known as, say, Paris, and it's a lot more inviting. For more than a dozen years, cross-country skiers have flocked here for America's biggest Nordic race, the American Birkebeiner. Somehow more than 15,000 skiers and spectators manage to squeeze into the area for what has developed into the skiing equivalent of the Kentucky Derby: one race and a whole lot of partying.

Perhaps it's because of the harsh winters and lack of urban entertainment, but folks who live in this part of the world have a special affinity for off-beat, challenging sports. They greeted the phenomenon of the Birkebeiner with great enthusiasm. After handling over 50,000 contestants in 13 years, these people know how to put on a race.

So it only makes sense that when a group of all-terrain bicycle fans decided to throw a race of their own, it would be done right. It was 3 years ago that Phil Van Valkenburg and Gary Crandall, both charter members of the slightly gonzo Chequamegon (pronounced She-mama-gun) Mamas Bicycle Club – which takes its name from a local national forest – launched a weekend Fat Tire

Illustration 1-1. A New England tenderfoot finds off-road racing to be a real scream.

Festival, confident they had the perfect course. Right in their backyard, the Birkebeiner ski trail cut a wide swath through ideal ATB terrain. It features grass, gravel, dirt, plenty of rolling hills, and more curves than an Argentine conga line.

"You've got to come out and race this thing," my friend Tom Kelly, a Hayward native and skiing promoter extraordinaire, crowed in a phone call to me. "National champ Joe Murray will be here. It's going to be the Midwest National Off-Road Bicycle Association (NORBA) Championships, and the Chequamegon Mamas are getting ready!"

"But Tom," I told him, trying to sound calm though I was already hooked, "I've never ridden an ATB."

"Picky, picky. The race isn't until the middle of September. You've got over a month to learn."

At the time it seemed reasonable, but as I found myself early one Saturday morning on the main street of Hayward preparing for the Chequamegon's parade start, I was beginning to have my doubts. "I Ride With Death," proclaimed the jerseys of a hard-looking team in front of me.

Head "Mama" Crandall was in front of the start line, going over a few details. "Now this year we've eliminated the long stretch over the railroad bed."

"That was a real killer," one of the Death Riders mumbled with a smile.

"Bought it bad there last year," his friend nodded, both sounding decidedly disappointed they were going to miss such delights.

"We have markers out there," Crandall continued, "warning you about any deep ruts you might want to avoid."

"As opposed to the ones we don't want to avoid," a woman next to me countered. She was wearing a Chequamegon Mamas jersey so I figured she must be a veteran.

"Tell me, what's this thing really like?" I asked nervously.

"It's long," she said, just as the gun went off, "but hard."

The Strategy: Full Tilt

It was during the parade start through town, following a Hayward police car to the beginning of the Birke trail, that I began to realize I had made a basic equipment mistake. I was riding a Montaneus made in nearby St. Cloud, Minnesota, a fast, strong bike noted for its adjustable head angle. But concerned about traction, I had chosen wide 2.25 tires and left them underinflated for a better grip. It was the setup I had been training on in Maine, and I knew it could climb like a hungry mule heading for the barn, but I hadn't predicted just how much speed I was sacrificing for grip – not until women and children started passing me. Right then I decided I would have to hit the hills full tilt to compensate for what I would lose on the straightaways.

On the outskirts of Hayward, the police car pulled to the side, and the lead riders peeled off into the high grass of the Birke trail. The Team Fisher boys were bunched together – Murray, "Jammin'" Jim Deaton, and George Theobald – with local hero Mark Frise of La Crosse, last year's winner, leading the way.

"It's been cut recently," Crandall had said of the trail, smiling, "but there's still a little grass out there." Right. And what a sudden, sharp drop in speed it causes after the smooth asphalt.

Now everybody is out of the saddle, cranking away up the first long hill. The Birke trail is cut wide enough to handle eight or nine skiers abreast, and I pull out of the pack to ride along the side, determined to make headway. The Montaneus responds beautifully, and by the crest of the hill I've passed more than a dozen riders.

The only problem is, I'm dead. Lungs burning. Beat. I tell myself it's always this way at the beginning of a race. The first few miles are the toughest, then you hit a rhythm, start feeling better. But I'm still sucking wind when the descent suddenly narrows, twisting around in a sharp turn, and the bike starts bucking like the mechanical steer at Gilley's Bar. Obviously this stretch of trail has been bombed, I think, trying to hold on as I slam in and out of potholes. And then I was airborne, about to become part of the trail.

Thirty-nine miles to go.

God Bless Chocolate Chip Cookies

Having never been in an off-road race, I had wondered if there would be anything like the team tactics or pack riding of a road race. But by the time I pulled into the first feed station at 10 miles, any semblance of a pack had long been replaced by something closer to the Bataan death march on bikes. Picture close to 300 riders in a bizarre assortment of garb, from racing shorts to jeans, jolting through the woods on fat tires, every man – or woman – for himself. Up front, Murray and Deaton might be blocking and drafting, but about 15 or 20 minutes off the lead, we were flat-out surviving.

And having one hell of a good time in the process. It was a perfect fall day, cool and crisp. The leaves were breaking out in gold and yellow. The riding was first-rate, hard and fun, almost constantly up and down with a mud patch waiting at the bottom of most hills. You'd reach the summit, spot the brown stuff, and swear that this time you were going to do it right – put the hammer down and hit the goo and water with enough speed to carry you through and up the other side. But look out . . . there's a keeper rut on the left . . . another bike blasting through on the right . . . can't brake much or it's dipsy doo time . . . speed's increasing . . . here comes the mud! . . . WHAMMO!

By the second rest stop, 20 miles in, I was feeling good, just a little beat-up with a few warning signs of fatigue. But I felt like the course had taken its best shot and I was still coming. We broke out of the woods, doglegged for a mile or so on an asphalt road (did that ever feel strange), and suddenly there was a long stretch of good gravel. Time to crank big gears and build some speed. Twenty, 22, 25 miles. This was a piece of cake. Be home before you know it.

I should have known better. I'd skied the Birke and I knew, absolutely knew, there was a stretch of gut-busting hills on the back half. But somehow my giddy, oxygen-depleted brain forgot. I felt positively betrayed when all at once we were back on the roller coaster, up and down, mud and sand, ruts and rocks. Curses and grinding derailleurs filled the air. The morning's energy had worn off, and I could feel the rough edge of my fatigue rubbing inside me like maladjusted gears. Cramps rippled my legs, and it seemed I had been riding this vibrating, shuddering contraption for most of my life.

I glanced at my watch: 12:30 P.M., 2½ hours since the start. I was just past 30 miles. They're probably drinking champagne at the finish, I thought bitterly, trying hard as I could to remember why I ever thought this might have been fun.

Like an oasis, there was a feed station. I stumbled in, and the experienced crew had just what I needed, some solid food – a doughnut, a couple bananas, and some big chocolate chip cookies. I took a moment to raise my seat, hoping the change would thwart the cramps, then wobbled off. There was a survivalist feeling in the air as everyone traded encouragement for the final haul. "Not much longer now . . . just a few more miles . . . only up around the bend . . . "

The seat adjustment helped, so did the food, and now it was fun again. A little flicker of satisfaction began to glow inside. The loudspeaker at the finish filtered through the woods, and then – how amazing – there were spectators and banners. "Field sprint to the line," a fellow next to me joked and, what the heck, we picked it up, laughing as we passed under the "Chequamegon Finish!" banner.

Second Helpings

Of course, the Fat Tire Festival wasn't nearly finished. As I limped out of bed the next morning, I realized – with only a slight shudder – that during the next 8 hours I could still take part in the "Rough Stuff Rendezvous," an orienteering competition on ATBs that sent bikers scrambling into the woods with a compass and map; the "Cable Criterium," a hilly beast of a race that included a mandatory jump and a lakeside hairpin turn; and the world-famous "Chequamegon Huffy Toss," in which contestants strain to see exactly how far they can throw – you guessed it – a Huffy bicycle.

The thought of spending the morning lost in the woods deterred me from entering the Rendezvous. As for the criterium, well, it sounded like so much fun to watch I didn't want to spoil the view. The Huffy Toss, however, seemed like my kind of event. I mean, I may not have the stringy, muscular build of a top cyclist, but I can bench 275 pounds.

Alas, there are some world-class Huffy tossers in the Wisconsin woods. My meager 26-foot heave was well off the winning

38-foot effort. "I just wanted to beat that little Huffy to death," the victor confided afterwards.

As can be expected, all this backwoods craziness produced a festive afterglow for the awards banquet. Hometown favorite Mark Frise had successfully defended his title in the 40-mile feature. Joe Murray had buried the competition in the criterium. His teammates Deaton and Theobald had taken their share of seconds and thirds.

Surprisingly, it was not Frise who received the most applause from the rowdy banquet crowd. That honor went to the three Team Fisher riders. Everyone from race organizers to spectators seemed delighted they had made the long trek from California to enter the race. The trio appeared somewhat overwhelmed by the warmth of the reception, but their real surprise came when race official Crandall inducted them into the ranks of the Chequamegon Mamas.

Illustration 1-2. They let loose with a raucous and heartfelt cry . . .

Want to Get into the Act?

If you get wind of locally organized races, that's probably a good place to start. You can also take part in races sanctioned by the National Off-Road Bicycle Association (NORBA), the organizing body for mountain bike racing. Any midpriced, stock fat-tire bike (that's $300 and up, in 1987 prices) should be able to handle most events.

NORBA races require a hardshell helmet, gloves, and working front and rear brakes – plus membership in NORBA; the annual membership fee is $25. To join or to ask for their schedule of races, write: NORBA, P.O. Box 1901, Chandler, AZ 85244.

"Now, boys," he said, handing over their new team jerseys while the crowd hooted, "you understand that to be a true Chequamegon Mama we need to hear you shout, 'Mama!' "

For a moment all three looked slightly desperate, as if they were wondering why they had ever left Marin County. But then they tilted back and let loose with a raucous and heartfelt call of Chequamegon.

I found myself yelling with them.

Roadies and Mudders Go Head-to-Head over Fitness

The house lights dim and the audience hushes. In the beam of a single smoky spotlight, a tuxedoed emcee strides to the middle of the ring and grabs a dangling microphone.

"Ladies and gentlemen," he drawls, "welcome to the ultimate showdown in the world of bicycle racing.

"In this corner, wearing sunglasses and weighing 160 pounds, from Aspen, Colorado, please welcome Olympic Road champion Alexi Grewal."

Photograph 1-3. Maybe you can't really compare the two, but the argument over the relative conditioning benefits of road racing and mountain-bike racing rages on.

With the roar of the crowd, the spindly 6-footer takes a casual step forward and waves.

"And in this corner, the 5-foot-8, 140-pound champion from the San Francisco Bay area. Let's hear it for National Off-Road champion Joe Murray."

Murray, shy as he is, acknowledges the enthusiastic applause with a simple nod and a half-smile.

What is this? A dream? A joke? Some Las Vegas invention to attract bicycle-riding high rollers?

No, it's an illustration of an argument that's been raging in U.S. cycling for some time – the debate over who's fitter, a top road racer like Grewal or a great off-road rider like Murray. Or, more precisely, which kind of bicycle racing builds fitness better, road or off-road?

Obviously, there are many differences between these two styles of cycling – equipment, road surface, average speed, and racers' attitudes and life-styles. What we're most concerned with, however, is the physical demands each places upon a rider. This is where the rift between roadies and mountain bikers is often the widest. Start comparing cardiovascular fitness, upper- and lower-body strength, or endurance, and you're guaranteed an entertaining prizefight.

Round One: Matters of the Heart

Cycling experts agree that road racers have better cardiovascular development than their off-road counterparts. In other words, their hearts tend to be stronger and their lungs capable of processing more oxygen per minute.

Steve Tilford, a National Road team member and also an accomplished mountain bike racer, goes so far as to say if there were ever a laboratory comparison between the two, the roadies would "kill 'em cardiovascularly."

"Top road racers like Grewal have been serious athletes for years," admits Gary Fisher of Fisher MountainBikes in San Rafael, California, "whereas guys like Murray are pioneers. For road racers, all those years of training have brought superior aerobic fitness and endurance."

Consider also the nature of road racing. In its ultimate form, the European professional circuit, it is a series of 1-day classics and major stage races marked by 150- to 180-mile events lasting 6 to 8 hours. European pros race five to seven times a week from early March through October. That's a total of 100 or more racing days every year.

Even top U.S. amateurs, who may compete 60 to 80 times a season in events as short as 50 miles, spend more time training than ATB specialists. These long hours on the bike, usually spent spinning the pedals, are what build cardiovascular fitness. In contrast, elite mountain bikers race an average of 25 times a season or about twice a week from May through September. Their typical event lasts 2 to 3 hours, spans 30 to 50 miles, and demands mostly short, anaerobic bursts of energy.

Not surprisingly, because of their cardiovascular edge, road racers have been able to overcome their lack of off-pavement experience and dominate many ATB events. "Cardiovascular fitness is why I won the [1984] NORBA Nationals," says Tilford. Other roadies who have used their strong lungs and hearts to fare well in such races include Dale Stetina, Gavin Chilcott, and Mark Frise.

But of late, the cardiovascular gap appears to be closing. ATB racers are training harder and longer and are showing improved aerobic fitness. In fact, roadies rarely win an off-road race any more. Grewal dropped out of the only one he ever entered, the 1984 NORBA Nationals, sporting a broken bike and a sprained sense of pride.

"Off-road racing is getting a lot more competitive," says Murray. "I used to be by myself most of the time, either breaking away or chasing someone. Now, there are usually several guys with me."

Round Two: Making Muscle

Total fitness involves more than cardiovascular endurance, however. It also entails upper-body strength and, in this area, off-road riders appear to have the advantage. Controlling the bike on a steep descent that is strewn with boulders, making thousands of subtle and not so subtle steering adjustments – these maneuvers develop the shoulders, lower arms, and hands.

Off-road racing also does more to promote lower-body or leg strength than conventional road racing. The most successful ATB riders are powerful pistons who excel on even the nastiest of inclines. Admittedly, part of this hill-climbing talent comes from cardiovascular fitness and part from a favorable strength-to-weight ratio, but a key factor is the strong leg muscle that off-road riding builds. In fact, many road racers are encouraged by their coaches to ride mountain bikes in the off-season for just this reason.

"If you consider general all-around fitness, ATB racers have an edge," says Tilford. "Road cyclists are so refined. Most of us are

Photograph 1-4. Off-road riding builds leg strength. And it's just what a bored roadie needs to put a smile on her face.

like thoroughbred race horses. We're unbelievably good at what we do – racing – but don't ask us to pull a plow because we'd pull a tendon or something."

Although riding off-road promotes overall body strength, it does have its liabilities. "It's like basketball," says Fisher. "You're an acrobat, constantly changing your position on the bike. You get a real thrashing. Your hands, your lower arms, and back really get beat up. It's hard to ride a lot of off-road races and recover. But you can road race several times a week, even every day, and get stronger, not weaker."

The Decision

After meeting the combatants and weighing their arguments, we await the decision of the judges. Which kind of racing builds fitness better? Which is the tougher kind of racing? It's hard to imagine anything more difficult than a European Pro Road Classic (typically through mud and over cobbles) or the 3-week Tour de France. Nevertheless, a 3-hour off-road race is 100 percent individual effort with the result being a physically shattered bicycle racer.

"A road rider can learn to handle ATB racing, its bike skills, its stress on the lower back and arms," says Tilford. "But it might take years for the off-road guys to learn to do what we do . . . maybe they couldn't."

Although it would be an interesting experiment, neither Murray nor Grewal is very excited about dabbling in the other's forte. Murray did some road racing this year but dropped out of his first few races, more from tactical bewilderment than fatigue. "I think I could eventually do well in road racing," he explains. "But for me it isn't as exciting as mountain bike racing. I like being out in the woods, where there aren't any cars and there's a real variety of terrain."

Meanwhile, Grewal dismisses his one, ill-fated off-road adventure, saying, "I'm not sure I'll ride any more mountain bike races. I really didn't enjoy it."

So, for the moment, Grewal remains a top road racer and Murray, an off-road ironman. Both are extremely fit at what they do, but their pursuits are significantly different. Who's to say which one's sport has made him fitter?

"The 'Who's Fitter?' argument doesn't hold water," says Ed Burke, Ph.D., former director of sports medicine, science, and technology for the U.S. Cycling Federation. "You can't compare apples to oranges. You can't compare Alexi Grewal to Joe Murray. Both are excellent athletes . . . and both are doing good things for bicycle racing. But there's the issue of specificity of training and it's crucial."

One thing about these two cyclists and their particular styles of racing can be compared, however. The exhausted look of a withered Grewal during Milan-San Remo, and the dirt-caked countenance of a bruised Murray following Crested Butte. Both are indicative of athletes who have given their all – two-wheeled warriors who will shower, eat, and then seek a rich reward of well-deserved sleep. Ladies and gentleman, we'll have to call this one a draw.

Part Two
Equipment to Suit Every Taste and Budget

The ABCs of Buying an ATB

All-terrain bikes don't just *look* different – they *are* different. Which means even the most knowledgeable road cyclist isn't necessarily prepared to shop for an ATB.

If you're about ready to grab your checkbook and head for the bike shop, that's great. But first, there are a few things you must know to select the proper bike.

Frame Size

For better ground clearance, the bottom bracket on a mountain bike is an inch or more higher than it is on a road bike. Thus, the frame size (measured along the seat tube) must be at least that much shorter. Unless you plan to ride only on paved roads, however, you'll need an additional inch or 2 of clearance between your crotch and the top tube. This is because off-road cycling often requires hopping off the pedals to prevent a fall. Thus, your ATB's seat tube should be 2 to 4 inches shorter than on a properly fitted road bike.

If you're unsure about the exact frame size, opt for the smaller one. Thanks to extralong seatposts, you'll still be able to achieve your optimum pedaling height. Plus, the lower the top tube, the farther you'll be able to drop your seat (using the quick-release mechanism) for extra stability on treacherous descents.

Handlebar Reach

The rules normally used to determine ideal top tube and stem length for road bikes don't apply to ATBs. In fact, for a given frame size, the distance between seat and handlebar can vary by an inch or more between models.

Although there is no consensus, race-oriented bikes generally stretch out the rider more than leisurely designs. The only way to find your ideal reach, however, is by experimenting with different models. As with drop-bar road bikes, substituting a longer or shorter stem can help fine-tune reach, but most production ATB stems are available in only one or two sizes. If the bike in question uses one-piece, triangulated Bullmoose-type

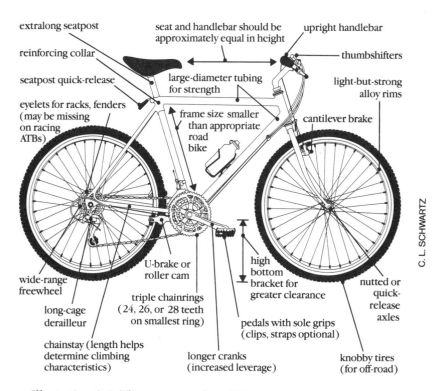

extralong seatpost

reinforcing collar

seatpost quick-release

eyelets for racks, fenders (may be missing on racing ATBs)

seat and handlebar should be approximately equal in height

large-diameter tubing for strength

frame size smaller than appropriate road bike

upright handlebar

thumbshifters

light-but-strong alloy rims

cantilever brake

wide-range freewheel

long-cage derailleur

chainstay (length helps determine climbing characteristics)

U-brake or roller cam

triple chainrings (24, 26, or 28 teeth on smallest ring)

longer cranks (increased leverage)

high bottom bracket for greater clearance

pedals with sole grips (clips, straps optional)

nutted or quick-release axles

knobby tires (for off-road)

C. L. SCHWARTZ

Illustration 2-1. The anatomy of an ATB.

bars, you'll have to replace the whole unit (at greater expense) to change the reach.

Riding position can also be modified by adjusting the handlebar so it's either more upright or sweeps farther back. Shortening wide bars with a hacksaw or pipe cutter can make an ATB more comfortable, too. We've seen bars on some production ATBs as wide as 32 inches, which results in a riding position most appropriate for Good Friday. Find your ideal width by gradually moving your hands closer together while riding. Many off-road experts prefer bars with 22- to 25-inch widths.

Frame Geometry

There's little agreement among mountain bike manufacturers as to the best frame angles, so expect to see many different designs. But, as is true with road bikes, the most agile ATBs have short wheelbases (around 42 inches), short chainstays (less than 17.5 inches), and steep head tube angles (70 to 71 degrees).

Such a configuration aids climbing by positioning the rider more directly over the rear wheel (improving traction), as well as providing responsive steering at slow climbing speeds. Often, the best-climbing ATBs are racing models with ultratight, sub-17-inch chainstays. Their only drawback is that such a tight rear end usually doesn't provide enough clearance for wide 2.125-inch tires. This is why some racing models come with narrow rubber. Check the clearance of the tires you plan to use, front and rear, before deciding.

Some sport ATBs (typified by the early model Stumpjumper) feature longer chainstays (up to 18.5 inches), a stretched out 43-to 44-inch wheelbase, and a slacker 68- or 69-degree head angle. These bikes are more stable on fast descents, more comfortable on bumpy roads, but less agile.

Our advice? Try riding both extremes to see which you prefer. If neither is to your liking, split the difference with a bike having 17.5- to 18-inch chainstays, a 69- or 70-degree head angle, and a 42.5-inch wheelbase. These approximate the specs for the typical sport ATB.

An ATB's seat tube angle has little effect on handling or rider comfort, but it does affect pedaling efficiency. The theory behind the shallow 68- to 70-degree angles found on some ATBs is that mountain bikers pedal more slowly and powerfully than roadies. Allowing you to sit farther back in the so-called "power position," facilitates this.

Although such geometry is well suited for steep climbs, it forces you to perch uncomfortably on the saddle nose when spinning. Most ATB designers now agree the seat tube angle that works best approximates that of a road bike.

Crank Length

Because the terrain is often steep and the cadence slow, an off-road cyclist needs longer cranks. For instance, the midsize rider who turns 170mm cranks on a 21- to 23-inch road bike will be best served by the 175mm cranks found on most 19- to 20-inch ATBs. Big riders who require a 22-inch or larger ATB can easily use 180mm cranks, although few bikes come with this size.

Form Follows Function

With that out of the way, it's shopping time. Keep in mind you want to buy a bike suited for the way you plan to use it. Just as with road bikes, most ATBs are designed with a specific purpose in mind – general sport riding, off-road racing, expedition touring, or center-city commuting.

Even so, there's much more crossover among mountain bikes than there is with road bikes. Thus, a single off-road model can play a variety of roles, especially if it's a sport bike. This general-purpose machine, comprising the bulk of the ATB market, is the practical choice for virtually all first-time off-roadies.

Most quality ATB frames are made of chrome-moly steel or (increasingly) aluminum. In either case, the tubing will likely be of a larger diameter than in the typical road frame. This is for added strength. Among steel road bikes, the lug work is an indicator of quality, but most ATBs are built without lugs, using either machine welds or, for more costly models, hand welding or fillet brazing. If done correctly, each of these methods results in a strong frame. On some high-quality, fillet-brazed bikes, seams are not even visible.

Whatever the price, your ATB will likely come with smooth-working derailleurs and brakes, thanks to advances in component technology. Most models feature indexed shifting, a godsend for new riders short on technique. As for brakes, some city models may still employ sidepulls, but all serious off-road machines use either cantilevers, SunTour roller cams, or Shimano or DiaCompe U-brakes. When properly adjusted, all are capable of locking a wheel with a two-finger squeeze. If you'll be riding a lot in the mud, choose cantilevers because they collect less glop.

If you want to use toe clips and straps, look for pedals that will accept them. Most ATB pedals have gripping surfaces on both sides, allowing you to maneuver over tricky spots with the clips hanging down and your feet ready to dab.

Sealed bearings in hubs, pedals, bottom brackets, and headsets have become common, even in less expensive ATBs. They simplify maintenance and protect against the ravages of dirt, mud, and creek crossings. Bolt-on hub axles, once considered necessary, are gradually being replaced by the more convenient quickrelease kind, which has proven its strength in off-road racing.

Also important is tire choice. Full knobbies work best in the dirt but buzz annoyingly on pavement. By contrast, all-purpose tires grip well in the dirt, yet provide a quiet ride on the road. Contrary to popular belief, *all* ATB tires, from skinny 1.4-inch road rubber to the obese 2.125s, will seat on *all* ATB rims. In fact, using fat tires on narrow rims makes the tire profile more round, thus increasing flotation and rim protection. Be careful, though, if you use narrow 1.5- to 1.75-inch tires on the widest, 32mm, rims. With more of the tire tucked beneath the rim flanges, there's less to absorb shock. Although such a combination works okay on the road, it isn't recommended for rough terrain.

Whatever Purpose You Have in Mind

Touring bikes are a subcategory of sport ATBs. The exact frame geometry is less important than the bike's sturdiness and its ability to handle a heavy load. The ideal off-road bike for extended touring has chainstays long enough to let your heels clear the rear panniers. Braze-on mounts for front and rear racks are a convenience, but their absence shouldn't eliminate a bike from consideration, because clamp-on racks are available. Although low-mount front racks are usually desirable because of their stability, such positioning on rugged terrain may result in the front bags scraping rocks or brush. Braze-ons for multiple water bottle cages are also important for long tours.

Although few production mountain bikes come with drop handlebars, some off-road tourists prefer them. They cite a more efficient riding posture and a greater variety of hand positions. Retrofitting drop bars requires using a longer stem that has less forward extension. A few ATB makers, notably Ross, use a smaller 0.833-inch-diameter steerer tube that won't accept a standard 22.2mm stem. Nitto offers an inexpensive high-rise "Technomics" stem in both steerer sizes.

Around-town ATBs are really modified mountain bikes. Although they're strong enough to hop curbs, they lack aggressive knobby tires, extra-stout tubing, and heavy-duty componentry common on the true dirt machines. Many city ATBs offer only 10 or 12 gears instead of the usual 15 or 18 on off-road bikes. But unless you commute in hilly San Francisco, this isn't a drawback. It's the upright riding position and comfort that are most important.

Although any off-road bike, save a fancy racing model that lacks fender and rack attachments, will perform well downtown, a specially designed city ATB is your best value. They are usually inexpensive, and some well-made models even have a lower bottom bracket so you won't have to stretch so far to put a foot down at stoplights.

Finally, there's the racing mountain bike – the thoroughbred of the off-road stable. Like its road-racing cousin, the off-road racer is typically lighter, has quicker handling, and is somewhat more fragile than a general-purpose bike. Pedals fitted with toe clips and straps, a relatively close-ratio freewheel, and the lack of rack or fender eyelets are tip-offs that the bike is intended for racing.

As with other off-road bikes, frame angles vary among manufacturers. Some are laid-back for downhill stability, and others are steep for instant responsiveness in tight quarters. These upright bikes require more rider skill on descents, but climb like the dickens.

Because many racers acquire a new frame every season, tubing is often light gauge, favoring performance over durability. Wheels are also expendable, and some of the lightest ATB rims and tires rival the weight of sturdy road equipment. All this pound shedding makes for a quick, responsive, and expensive bike. Although everyone should have the pleasure of riding an aggressive, 25-pound racing ATB at least once, few first-time buyers can justify the hefty price. Nevertheless, once you've raced the wind on a thoroughbred, it's tough to climb back on a plowhorse. And that's why there are a lot more hot racing ATBs out there than there are off-road racers.

The Bikes Have Never Been Better

Mountain bikes, ATBs, fat-tire bikes, clunkers, dirt bikes – call them what you will, they're here to stay. And if you're about to go out and buy one, your timing is terrific. The quality of bike for the buck has never been greater, as those who paid $750 for an original, 1981 Stumpjumper can attest. Not to take anything away from this classic, but ATBs that ride better, stop quicker, and shift more precisely are now available for less than half that price.

To prove it, we took a look at five of 1987's great buys. The most expensive sold for $575, while the least costly was just under $300. All are ideal for street riding, occasional forays in the dirt, and even serious excursions into the outback.

Schwinn Sierra

The problem with a fancy ATB paint job is it doesn't look fancy for long. You can take pride in the scratches and chips, or you can protect the finish by riding so conservatively you never crash and burn (or have any fun). Or you can own an ATB with a finish as bombproof as its wheels and frame – the Schwinn Sierra, with an 1987 suggested retail price of $369.

When we completed our off-road test and washed the Sierra, its black chrome finish was still immaculate. The smoky, muted gloss contrasts with the glitter of bright chrome, glowing more like polished pewter than a simonized Chevy bumper. The Sierra also comes painted red with white component highlights.

The durable chrome finish is our choice, because this bike loves to be taken into the woods and abused. In step with what makes a sweet-handling ATB, Schwinn redesigned the Sierra with a shorter wheelbase (42½ inches) and chainstays (17½ inches), a steeper head angle (69 degrees), and 2 inches of fork rake. Chrome-moly tubing throughout, including oversized, double-butted main tubes, bolsters the Sierra's survivability while holding the weight to 29½ pounds for our 19-inch test bike.

As you'd expect from these numbers, the Sierra is easy to ride. It's suitable for gonzo sport riding, and thanks to dual front and rear dropout eyelets for fenders and racks, it's ideal for commuting or touring.

Although it's not a high-performance bike, the Sierra climbs reasonably well. Substituting a handlebar with less (or no) rise would help the front wheel stay grounded on steep ascents, but the bike's "heads-up" riding position may be more important to ATB newcomers.

On descents, the Sierra feels stable, balanced, and brake-slides through turns with aplomb. This maneuver is easy to initiate with the lightly lugged Schwinn Terra tires and venerable Shimano AT50 cantilever brakes, which stop almost as well as fancy roller cams and U-brakes but are lighter and collect less mud.

The dirt/pavement tires are the Sierra's weak point. Off road, a thick, raised center ridge hinders traction. On pavement, this ridge causes disconcerting squirm in turns as it and the side lugs vie for road contact. Fortunately, better tires are widely available (see "Time to Re-Tire?" later in this part of the book) and the frame can accept the fattest.

Shimano Light Action derailleurs provide positive front shifts and SIS rear changes that let you click-and-forget even while driving hard out of the saddle. The levers also allow conventional friction shifting, a vital feature for any indexed off-road gear system, which can be rendered useless by a crash-damaged derailleur hanger. By switching to the friction mode you can ride the Sierra home, tweak its hanger into line, and have nothing to show for your crash – not even a paint scratch.

Supergo Access

Okay, off-road warriors, price this ATB: Its oversized Columbus tubing is neatly TIG-welded and features a seat tube ovalized at the bottom bracket for lateral rigidity. It has a Shimano Deore indexed gear system. The powerful front cantilever brake is supplemented by a massive U-brake under the chainstays. Biopace chainrings are standard, as are strong Araya RM25 rims shod with genuine Ritchey Quad tires. Fancy touches include a chrome-moly Salsa roller stem, toe clips and straps, and a nifty little shoulder strap that doubles as a tool bag. Is your guess $600 or $700? More?

Not even close. This is the $499 Supergo Access. It's made in Taiwan of Columbus Matrix seamed tubing – but unlike a few years ago, there's no onus to either Formosan manufacturing or tubing that started as flat strips. So what's the catch? The Access is available only from Bikecology, a mail-order company. You can't cruise around the parking lot before you buy, and you're responsible for assembly, which requires an adjustable wrench, a 6mm Allen key, and the mechanical savvy to use them correctly.

Our sample came with the rear wheel installed, clips and straps attached, and gears and brakes perfectly adjusted. We had to install the front wheel, bar/stem, seatpost, seat, and pedals, and inflate the tires. The whole process took about 20 minutes.

Bicycling's test circuit consists of 2 miles of pavement to a steep, single dirt track, followed by a rolling bridle path that leads to abrupt climbs with rocky descents. A log or two along the way keeps our trials riding sharp.

The Access got A's on all sections. On pavement, the Ritchey Quad's center ridge of offset knobs is surprisingly quiet for a tire with the tenacity to conquer dirt and mud. At 80 pounds per square inch (psi) they roll fast, too. At the trailhead we bled half their air and attacked the first ascent. We appreciated the long, low 10 centimeter reach of the Salsa bar and stem. It made it easy to weight the front wheel for control even while sitting back to enhance rear-wheel traction. The extension also kept the bar clear of churning knees when we stood. The 17½-inch chainstays help traction by putting the rear wheel more directly under the body.

The liberal stem extension also acts as a tiller to improve control. It makes slow-speed steering akin to high-speed steering, which is done not by turning the handlebar but by leaning the upper body. Shorter stems provide less leverage and require more strength and concentration to maintain a straight path through ruts and rocks. The more fork rake a bike has (and the

Access has a generous 2¼ inches to provide adequate trail with its 69.5-degree head angle), the greater the front wheel's tendency to be deflected by obstacles, especially at slow speeds.

The up side of this head angle-rake combination is apparent on the downside of a hill. ATBs with steeper head angles and less rake can get scary on blazing descents, but the Access's moderate front end inspires confidence. This tester, having grown accustomed to his own bike with a 71-degree head and 1.9 inches of rake, was amazed how much safer he felt while descending at the same speed on the Access.

With the Ritchey Quads daringly deflated to 30 psi, the Access handled the bumpiest trails with minimal jostling. For ultimate pampering we installed a pair of 2.02 Fisher FatTrax tires, the widest, smoothest-riding off-road rubber. They cleared the forks and stays with about 5mm to spare, but the lugs came within 3mm of the rear U-brake – close enough to cause mud buildup.

One equipment note: the Salsa chrome-moly roller stem is stock on the Access, but our test bike's flat Salsa handlebar is not. Bikecology's Alan Goldsmith explained that the Nitto bar he specified was not available for our sample. Although a flat bar helps produce a low position for competitive riding, most riders will probably appreciate the slightly more upright posture afforded by the Nitto, which has a 4 centimeter rise.

Raleigh Elkhorn

Tech talk is fine, but sometimes you have to throw away the tape measure, trash the angle finder, and just enjoy the ride.

A case in point is Raleigh's new Elkhorn, an emerald green, $510 to $560 sport ATB that rides like a bike that is twice as expensive. Although this is great for you and Raleigh, we're at a loss to explain it.

Most of the specs are perfectly normal – 2 inches of fork rake, 69.5-degree head angle, 17½-inch chainstays. It's a fine, balanced design that splits the difference between steep-angled racing ATBs and long-wheelbase cruisers that need a ski lift to get uphill. Lots of ATBs share the Elkhorn's dimensions.

But there are a couple of quirks – a tight, 41-inch wheelbase and a low, 11⅛-inch bottom bracket. The former allows the rear wheel to quickly follow the front during sudden maneuvers, while putting the rider's weight squarely between the axles. The low bottom bracket keeps the center of mass closer to the dirt, for better control.

The Elkhorn also features oversized, triple-butted chrome-moly tubing, TIG welding, and an investment cast fork crown and seat lug cap. Sure, the frame feels stiff and responsive when charging up or down a steep hill, but we'd be lying if we said we could feel the difference between triple- and double-butted tubes.

Probably part of the reason this bike climbs and maneuvers so well has nothing to do with the frame. It's in the wheels. Just as light wheels are the best way to improve a road bike's performance, the Elkhorn's 485-gram Araya RM20 rims and 1.95-inch skinwall tires minimize critical rotating weight. The Raleigh-brand Taiwanese tires have offset center lugs for a quiet ride on pavement and adequate grip in dirt. Because the side lugs aren't deep, it's easy to slide through turns without the tires digging in and pitching you over the high side.

Shimano's new Deore off-road componentry gives the Elkhorn awesome braking and near-flawless shifting. Two-finger braking is the norm, and the rear derailleur can be upshifted or downshifted while jamming out of the saddle. Try this without indexed shifting and you'll appreciate the difference. The Elkhorn's front changer also performs extremely well, but, like every other front derailleur we've used except the top-line Deore XT, it requires a reduction in pedal pressure for downshifts.

To complete an already fine bike, Raleigh sweated the details, such as offering the Elkhorn with a compact, 16½-inch frame (measured center-to-top). Other nice touches include comfortable anatomic grips, a leather Viscount saddle; a spoke holder that protects the right chainstay; braze-ons for racks, fenders, and two bottles; Biopace chainrings; and sealed bearings even in the Victor pedals. These do not, however, accept toe clips and straps, nor do they match the quality of the rest of the bike.

Univega Rover Sport

Few ATB owners expect to race or explore a route through the Himalayas. Most just want an inexpensive, fun-to-ride bike to carry them to and from work on weekdays, and perhaps along peaceful, wooded park trails on weekends.

If you spell "gonzo" with a small "g" and don't care if the ATB you ride is the same model that once cracked Mach 1 under some Marin County hotshot, save some money by checking out Univega's Rover Sport. At $280 ($299 on East Coast) it was a best-buy ATB that's ideal for pavement and adequate for all but big-G maneuvers on dirt.

Not simply a disguised city bike, the yellow and black Rover Sport boasts many performance features of more costly earth movers. The triple crankset and 6-speed freewheel yield a gear range from 26 to 89 inches – high enough for cruising and low enough for mountain climbing. The 170mm cranks are fine for quick cadence on the street but a tad short for best leverage in the dirt. The pedals accept toe clips and straps, indispensable equipment on road or off, we feel.

The TIG-welded frame is composed of triple-butted chrome-moly with an oversized, 1⅜-inch down tube, 1⅛-inch top tube, and a beefy unicrown fork. During hard pedaling, the bottom bracket felt more unyielding than many light-gauge, high-performance ATBs we've ridden.

Of course, this admirable rigidity is achieved at the expense of weight. The Rover Sport's frame/fork weighs 7.75 pounds, and the complete bike totals 30.85 pounds (about 4 more than a racing ATB). Also discouraging high performance are the 18.25-inch chainstays, which position the rear wheel too far back for good traction on steep climbs. The Cheng Shin 1.5-inch, dual-purpose tires use offset center lugs for a quiet ride on pavement and fair traction on dirt roads. For serious off-road riding you'll want to substitute wider, more aggressive rubber.

Quick maneuvering isn't this bike's forte. The 43¾-inch wheelbase means the rear wheel takes time to realize where the front is going. Comfort is the up side of this expanse, with the rider suspended between the wheels on a shock-deadening frame. Helping matters is the wide, padded Vetta anatomic saddle. It's a good choice, because the bike's upturned handlebar provides a vertical riding position that concentrates weight on the seat. But if you like to ride hunched forward or if you have thick thighs, you may prefer a narrower saddle.

The Rover Sport's componentry corresponds well to the type of riding it's designed for. Sure-stopping Shimano AT50 cantilever brakes are matched with Shimano's new AT56 levers. These have an adjustable reach, a plus for the small hands that will control this bike's 16½-inch diamond and 17½-inch mixte models.

Shifting precision is courtesy of Light Action SIS. This system ranks third in Shimano's price structure, but it's close in performance to top-line Deore XT. The rear derailleur, for instance, can can be upshifted and downshifted under load – even while standing on the pedals. It can also be clicked to the next higher or lower gear while coasting, and will shift flawlessly when pedaling is resumed. This is as useful in city traffic as in the boonies.

Boonies? Yes, the Rover Sport is adequate for real off-road riding. You might have to walk steep climbs, but this sub-$300 bargain will take you anywhere a more expensive ATB will – except to the poor house.

Fisher Hoo-Koo-E-Koo

No, Hoo-Koo-E-Koo is not the factory in Taiwan that builds Gary Fisher's most affordable mountain bike (they don't call 'em ATBs in Marin County). It's a Native American word meaning "Indians who live at base of Mount Tamalpais," the trail-crossed California peak upon which Fisher helped originate mountain biking.

If you're in the market for a spirited sport ATB (sorry, Gary), forget the history lesson. For you, the name means "Fisher quality, race-worthy geometry, bargain price." Yes, for only $575 (in 1987) you, too, could Hoo-Koo-E-Koo.

It's a funny name, but this is a serious bike, equal in design and performance to Fisher's American-made models with similar specs. Attention to the finer points of ATB design is evident from the slotted cable stops that simplify lubrication to the ovalized seat tube for bottom bracket stiffness. Rims are light-but-tough Araya RM20, the standard for high-performance off-road bikes.

To temper the price, Fisher specs the Hoo-Koo-E-Koo with Taiwanese HTI pedals and a nondescript-but-adequate 300mm alloy seatpost. There's no cost cutting, however, in the brake and gear systems, which come from Shimano's new Deore group. Low gear is a forgiving 24 inches (28-tooth chainring and 30T cog), and the bike's 96-inch high gear ensures plenty of go-power when tires meet pavement.

Under the standout Caribbean green paint, the frame is neatly TIG-welded of American-made True Temper chrome-moly tubing, using Fisher's new race geometry (69.5-degree head angle, 73.5-degree seat). For superb climbing traction the chainstays are a short 17 inches, but there's ample clearance for the wide Fisher FatTrax tires that came on our test bike. Future production will have 1.6-inch Fisher slicks, but the option of using wide rubber is appreciated.

Complementing the bike's well-balanced geometry is the long (10.5-centimeter), tall (11-centimeter) Fisher Rhino stem, a stiff chrome-moly fixture that uses a pulley cable guide like Salsa's premium Pro-Moto stem. Combining the long extension with a no-rise, 24-inch-wide steel handlebar lets the rider scoot back in the saddle for improved traction while keeping the front end weighted. The brake levers are always within reach, the bar's minimal rearward bend reduces uncomfortable wrist twist while climbing out of the saddle, and the long stem keeps everything clear of flailing knees.

The end result is a bike that feels as if it's an extension of the body. It comes as close to "disappearing beneath the rider" – the ultimate compliment usually reserved for road racing machines – as any ATB we've ridden.

Time to Re-Tire?

Changing the capabilities of your ATB is as easy as changing its tires. If you want to race off-road or explore trails, install knobby, high-performance rubber. If all of your riding is on pavement, go for a smooth-rolling street tire. And if you want to be ready for anything, opt for a combination tread.

The fact is, the tires that come on a new ATB may not perform well off-road. Often they are skinny and light because distributors pay a lower import tariff on bikes with tires narrower than 1.625 inches.

So, even if you are buying a new bike, you may also want to choose new tires. Five years ago this was a simple task, with just a handful of knobby off-road models to pick from. But as you can see in the table on pages 42-43, there are now a number of specialty tires. If you want to ride on ice and snow, for instance, the IRC Blizzard provides metal studs. If you need to carry a spare, there are foldable tires with a lightweight Kevlar bead. And if pavement is your thing, you can maximize rolling efficiency with a treadless model.

Of course, you must bear in mind any built-in limitations your bike's frame geometry, chainstay length, and the like might impose on intended use as you form your expectations of the performance of the new tires. (See "The ABCs of Buying an ATB" earlier in this part of the book.) That's not to negate what we've just said here about the role of rubber – just to aid you in being realistic.

To help you understand the choices and find the best tire for your type of riding, we've included these key characteristics in the table on pages 42-43.

Weight. We weighed all tires in our lab. Tire samples frequently vary by 20 grams or more, and it's rare for a tire to weigh exactly what the manufacturer claims. Lighter tires feel livelier and require less effort to pedal. Heavier tires are more capable of withstanding abusive terrain.

Size. You'll note a discrepancy between our laboratory findings and manufacturer claims. This is because there's no standard for measuring a tire's diameter and width. Says one industry insider, "I look at another company's advertised size and I don't know what it means because I don't know where they're measuring from. Those numbers are really meaningless."

We measured *diameter* with each tire inflated to 40 psi on a Specialized X28 rim. If you switch to tires with a diameter different from those you're riding, your bike's handling characteristics will change. For example, smaller-diameter tires produce quicker steering. Beware of installing two tires with different diameters. In effect, this changes the bike's head angle and, thus, its handling.

We measured *width* from sidewall to sidewall (or lug to lug, whichever was wider) at 40 psi. To determine whether you can switch to a wider model, check the clearance between your present tire and the chainstays. You must maintain a gap of several millimeters in case a wheel becomes out of true. In general, a narrow tire rolls faster and requires more pressure to

Photograph 2-1. Change the way your bike rides by changing the tires.

protect the tube and rim, and a wide tire absorbs more shock and "floats" over rough surfaces.

Inflation range. A wide range is preferable if you'll be mixing road and off-road riding. The more psi a tire can take, the more efficient it will be on pavement. The fewer psi it requires to avoid pinched-tube flats, the better it will perform on soft ground. Thus, you'll be able to ride briskly to the trailhead, bleed some air, and enjoy optimum off-road performance.

Tread type. There are three tread categories, which we call *off-road* (racing and trail riding), *road* (pavement), and *combination*. An off-road tire produces excessive rolling resistance and noise when ridden on pavement. A road tire lacks the traction and toughness necessary for rough terrain. A combination tire is a compromise, having a relatively smooth center section

(continued on page 44)

TABLE 2-1.
Buyers' Guide to ATB Tires

Brand	Model	Suggested Retail Price ($)	Advertised Weight (g)	Actual Weight (g)
AVOCET	FasGrip City 1.5	17.95	425	420
AVOCET	FasGrip City 1.9	17.95	565	643
CARLISLE	Aggressor R/T II	10.95	n/a	869
CHENG SHIN	Marin Pro Combo	11.95	n/a	679
CHENG SHIN	Marin Rockstar	17.95	655	615
FISHER	FatTrax	24.95	750	778
IRC	Racer X-1 Pro	8.95	680	683
IRC	Blizzard	19.95	910	929
KENDA	K 52	8	n/a	662
KENDA	K 60	8	n/a	812
MICHELIN	Hi-Lite Express	17	430 515	434
RITCHEY	Force Racing K	29.95	595	659
RITCHEY	Force Racing	19.95	675	698
RITCHEY	Force Duro K	29.95	645	578
RITCHEY	Force Duro	19.95	725	689
RITCHEY	Quad 1.9	19.95	675	748
SPECIALIZED	Hardpack 1.5	20	520	529
SPECIALIZED	Hardpack 2.2	20	780	640
SPECIALIZED	Ground Control	20	735	810
SPECIALIZED	Ground Control/S	20	600	555
SPECIALIZED	Crossroads II	20	650 530 500	643
SPECIALIZED	Fat Boy	18	345	329

Advertised Size (in.)	Actual Diameter (in.)	Actual Width (in.)	Inflation Range (psi)	Tread Type	Bead	TPI
26 × 1.5	25.19	1.38	50-85	road	steel	66
26 × 1.9	25.5	1.69	80	road	steel	66
26 × 2.10	25.75	1.63	65	combination	steel	35
26 × 2.0	26	1.75	35-45	off-road	steel	62
26 × 2.0	26.25	1.75	35-45	off-road	Kevlar	62
26 × 2.02	26.25	1.94	30-45	off-road	steel	70
26 × 2.0	25.75	1.75	45-80	off-road	steel	127
26 × 2.125	26.25	1.88	40-50	off-road (studded)	steel	66
26 × 1.75	25.38	1.5	40-65	combination	steel	62
26 × 1.9	25.75	1.31	45-65	off-road	steel	62
26 × 1.5 (26 × 1.75 also available)	25.13	1.38	60	off-road	Kevlar	n/a
26 × 1.9	26	1.69	45-80	off-road	Kevlar	127
26 × 1.9	26	1.69	45-80	off-road	steel	66
26 × 1.9	26	1.69	45-80	off-road	Kevlar	127
26 × 1.9	26	1.69	45-80	off-road	steel	66
26 × 1.9	25.88	1.75	45-80	off-road	steel	66
26 × 1.5	26.63	1.56	35-80	off-road	steel	66
26 × 2.2	26.5	1.94	35-80	off-road	steel	66
26 × 1.95	26.25	1.88	35-80	off-road	steel	66
26 × 1.95	26.13	1.81	35-80	off-road	Kevlar	66
26 × 1.95 (26 × 1.50, 24 × 1.50 also available)	26	1.75	35-80	combination	steel	66
26 × 1.25	24.75	1.25	100	road	steel	66

to reduce noise and rolling resistance on pavement, and surrounding tread to provide off-road traction. In general, this design does not work as well as those made specifically for each environment.

Bead. A tire has two, forming the inside circumference on each side. Most beads are steel wire, but Kevlar offers two advantages – lighter weight and pliability. A Kevlar-bead tire can be easily folded and packed into a saddle bag.

Threads per inch (TPI). A high number means thin fabric cords were used to construct the casing. Such a tire will be relatively flexible and efficient, but susceptible to cuts. A low number signifies thicker cords, which produce a heavier, stiffer, and stronger casing. The Michelin Hi-Lite Express features a weave-type casing, so TPI does not apply.

Finally, as you study the photo on page 41 you'll see a variety of tread designs. There is no objective way to evaluate perform-ance within each category. Much depends on how a tread corre-sponds with trail conditions in your area. For instance, tires with closely spaced knobs or lugs, while fine for dry conditions, tend to collect mud. Conversely, the Fisher FatTrax and Specialized Ground Control/S are examples of tires designed to release mud. And even some road tires have off-road applications. The Avocet FasGrip City is reportedly the tire of choice on the Slickrock Trail near Moab, Utah.

We recommend talking with experienced off-road riders and experts at local bike shops. Use their recommendations to select a tread for your climate and terrain.

The Right Stuff for Off-Road

We'd be kidding ourselves if we expected that every production-line or even custom-made mountain bike came fully equipped with all the accessories to suit our particular style of riding. And certainly there are additional accoutrements that would make the off-road experience all the more accessible and enjoyable.

So take a gander at some of the newer ATB accessories which we've tested out and found useful. They'll give you an idea of some of the gear available. Then sometime soon browse a bit through a good bike shop in your area that sells off-road gear, and perhaps you'll happen on a few "necessary" accessories. If something here suits your needs, ask about it at your bike shop. Also we've included addresses of manufacturers that welcome inquiries.

Vary Your Grip

Road cyclists find relief from hand and upper body fatigue by changing their position on the handlebars. ATB riders have had to make do with just one handgrip position – until now. The Moots Road Handles grips, from Moots Manufacturing, provide a welcome new hand and arm position that we found helps ease fatigue. The grips also make an aerodynamic, arms-tucked-in riding position easier to achieve. Made of stainless steel, wood, and firm foam padding, these grips are sturdy enough for hard use. Write to Moots Mfg., P.O. Box 2480, 1136 Yampa St., Steamboat Springs, CO 80477. But this is not the only new option for handlebars. Read on.

Get a Grip on Performance

Because of its unique shape, our testers found Jets ATB handlebar enhances power, control, and comfort. Upturned grips,

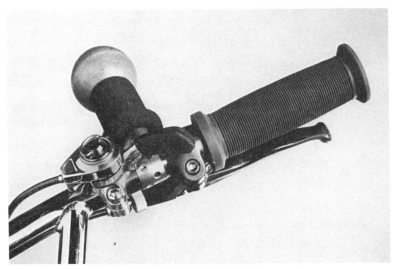

Photograph 2-2. Moots Road Handles – one option for changing your grip.

similar to a pursuit bike's, allow full use of the biceps when climbing. And compared to conventional ATB bars, Jets is also more comfortable and responsive on rough terrain. The curved bar is easy to grip and places hands and arms in a natural shock-absorbing position. We also like the option of riding with hands on the bar tops. Our Jets had contoured Grab-On foam grips, DiaCompe 283 downsize ATB levers, and SunTour bar-con shifters – an excellent combination. Regular thumbshifters may also be used. Jets won't fit into regular stems, so a two-piece model (Nitto MT-1, SunTour MS-1300, Specialized slingshot-type) or a custom stem must be used. Jets is made of ⅞-inch-diameter, TIG-welded chrome-moly tubing. Widths of 43 and 45.5 centimeters are available. Write to Jets, Box 805, Boulder, CO 80306.

Have It Both Ways

Having trouble choosing between an upright or drop-style handlebar for your ATB? Have it both ways with Grizzly Bars from DIDn, Inc. Grizzly Bars bolt onto conventional upright handle-bars between the grips and shift levers. They can be set in four positions, one of which duplicates that of drop handlebars. They

Photograph 2-3. Grizzly Bars give you drops *and* uprights.

are sturdy, easy to install, and provide a welcome option for those who ride on- and off-road, our testers say. On the downside, they add 21 ounces and place hands away from the brakes. Grizzlys fit handlebars up to ⅞ inch in diameter. Write to DIDn Inc., Box 1018, Biggar, SK, Canada S0K 0M0.

Shoulder Saver

When an unrideable obstacle looms, cyclocross riders and master off-roadies smoothly dismount while still moving, sling the bike onto a shoulder, and keep going at a run. It helps greatly to have a frame-mounted device to cushion the shoulder and stabilize the carry. The new Portage Pad from Moots Manufacturing features firm foam padding, a leather cover, and contoured fit. It takes the pain out of a shoulder carry, our testers found. A stainless steel band with a draw-up bolt assembly secures the unit to the bike. Mounting bands to fit top tubes from 1 inch to 1¼ inches in diameter are available. (Address on page 45.)

Stop Sprocket Eaters

ATBs are sturdy machines, but they have a "soft" component underneath that needs protection: the aluminum alloy chainrings. Hopping a rock or log can result in bent or broken chainring teeth. The Bashguard fends off such sprocket-eating obstacles. We were skeptical that a plastic part weighing only 6 ounces could take such a beating, but the Bashguard held firm after repeated hard hops onto and over rocks and logs. The mounting straps fit virtually any size tubing, including the fat Cannondale frames. Write to BSL Machining, 148 Los Molinos, San Clemente, CA 92672.

Mud-Slinging Shoes

There's fun to be had out in that winter mud – and a pair of off-road cycling shoes can help make mud-jamming a blast. The nylon/leather Cross model from Rivat of France has a high-traction sole, optional metal spikes, and supportive uppers that are sturdy and warm.

Photograph 2-4. Bashguard answers an S.O.S. (that's "Save Our Sprockets").

The slightly curved sole has just enough flexibility for comfortable running, yet enough stiffness to resist pressure from the pedals. A sawtooth pattern on the bottom grips the pedal nicely and offers traction when you must dismount. Under the heel, two soccer-style metal spikes can be installed when needed. The uppers are nylon mesh reinforced with leather. They extend well up the ankle for protection and support. The Cross can be ordered through your local bike shop.

Easy Shine

Many cyclists use a paste wax on their bicycle frames . . . once. That's all it takes to find out what a chore it is to clean dried, white wax out of lug edges, braze-ons, and other other hard-to-get-at bicycle crannies you just don't find on cars. But the new Professional Frame Wax is easily buffed away and leaves no unsightly residue. It does leave a nice shine. Professional Frame

Wax was developed for framebuilder Dave Moulton by Bike Elixir and is said to be safe for all metals and paints, including DuPont Imron. The wax is sold at many bike shops, or write to Bike Elixir, 1132 Mirabella Ave., Novato, CA 94947.

Jaws

If you've ever passed up some good sightseeing or a restaurant stop because your two-wheeled pride and joy couldn't be left unattended on a cartop rack, consider the Bikemaster from Macorex. This carrier features a rubber-cushioned, lockable alloy jaw that clasps the bicycle's bottom bracket. For extra security, an optional 54-inch-long, coated steel cable can be looped through the wheels and locked into the jaw mechanism.

The unit can be mounted on some standard crossbars, but we found that it works best with Macorex's own gutter lock-in Guardian rack. One disadvantage: the Bikemaster's locking jaws may not fit bikes with oversize aluminum tubing, or those with derailleur cable guides under the bottom bracket. Available from United Products, Inc., 135 West 36th St., New York, NY 10018.

Hide-Away Pump

It's not easy to carry a pump on an ATB. Even if you can find room, it often gets jarred loose or clogged with dirt. Wilderness Trail Bikes' internally mounted aluminum pump solves these problems. It fits snugly *inside* the seatpost and seat tube. When you need to inflate a spare, simply free the seatpost (most ATBs have a quick-release mechanism), remove the pump, and attach the built-in flexible hose with a Shraeder valve. The Wilderness Trail Bikes' pump weighs 3.6 ounces and fits inside seatposts with a minimum diameter of 0.875 inches. It may not pass the water bottle bosses of some seat tubes, however. To check yours, try inserting a dowel, 21mm in diameter, past the cage bosses. Bottle cage bolts can be cut or backed out and shimmed to provide the necessary clearance. Write to Wilderness Trail Bikes, 105 Montford Ave., Mill Valley, CA 94941.

Photograph 2-5. An internally mounted pump you can't lose.

A Better Bag

The new Frame Bag from Overland Equipment mounts neatly behind the head tube. It's handier than a behind-the-seat bag and more stable than a handlebar bag, because of its lower position and four-point mounting system. The 9-by-14-inch Frame Bag has two wide, zippered pockets and is made of rugged Cordura nylon with double-stitching at stress points. It's narrow enough for knee clearance while pedaling. The Frame Bag is available in three sizes (fits 18- to 24-inch frames). Write to Overland Equipment, Box 3255, Chico, CA 95927.

Tires with Bite . . . and Without

We charged through familiar turns faster than ever on an ATB equipped with Ground Control tires from Specialized and Wilderness Trail Bikes. One look at the knobbies bristling from this tire tells you it's made for the dirt. Unlike dual-purpose ATB tires, the 1.9-inch-wide Ground Control has no raised center ridge but a row of staggered tread blocks to provide bite. From center to sidewall, these blocks become progressively taller and narrower, which provides exceptional cornering traction and predictable sliding.

Quiet and fast on the road, grippy and aggressive in the dirt – that's the Quad 1.9 tire from Ritchey USA. A row of diagonally linked tread blocks provides a fast-rolling crown surface that has minimal rolling resistance and road hum, we found. But because there's no solid, slippery center rib, the tire gets good traction in the dirt, too.

Just when we thought we'd seen all the variations on the treadless tire, along came the FasGrip City from Avocet. No, it doesn't work in the dirt. We tried. But for someone who wants an extra set of wheels for road riding an ATB, the 80-psi FasGrip City makes sense. The glossy fat look is just right for ATBs that may never be ridden on anything rougher than a beach.

Bike or Hike Bag

Whether you're exploring city sights or mountain heights, a backpack is handy when you're off the bicycle. But you needn't take along a backpack and a pannier (bike bag), because the new Kalahari Mountain carrier from Karrimor can serve as either. This convertible bag looks and performs like a pannier, but unclip it from the rack, unzip a protective cover to reveal a set of padded packstrips – and you're ready for a hike. Matching, nonconvertible rear and front panniers are also available.

Karrimor built in the backpack feature without compromising the stability and usefulness of the pannier, we found. Yet it's comfortable as a backpack, too. The bag has a capacity of 1,200 cubic inches and features a top-opening main compartment, a deep 11-inch-wide outside pocket, and a mesh pocket on the top flap. The bag is made of coated, heavy-duty 1,000-denier nylon pack cloth, wide reinforcement panels, and double-stitching at stress points.

Gordon's ATB Rack

Low-mount front racks put the weight of the load where it belongs, but during off-road riding low-mount panniers can be destroyed by rocks and brush. The new ATB rack from Bruce Gordon Cycles solves the problem by providing 14 inches of ground clearance while keeping the center of the panniers near the steering axis. Gordon's rack is wide enough to clear cantilever brake arms, so a load can be mounted over them, rather than in front of them. The rack attaches at the front dropout eyelet and clamps to the upper fork arms. It has the same chrome-moly steel, machine mitered, hand-brazed construction as other Gordon racks. It proved extremely rigid during our test rides when loaded with panniers carrying a total of 25 pounds. Write to Bruce Gordon Cycles, 1070 West 2d St., Eugene, OR 97402.

Dirty Duds – All-Terrain Clothing Comes of Age

You wouldn't ride a lightweight racing bike on a rugged off-road trail, but you'd probably wear the same jersey and shorts. As you'll eventually discover when thorny brush turns your expensive togs into nylon/Lycra spaghetti, such clothes can't handle much off-road abuse.

Enter a new generation of all-terrain clothes. In a swiftly evolving category, manufacturers are attempting to create fashionable yet functional clothing that's easy to care for, comfortable, and most important, durable.

Consider, for example, the advantages of a pair of knickers with padded knees. These not only fend off trail debris better than conventional shorts, but also offer extra protection in case of a fall. Shorts for off-road riding have been fortified with sturdy fabric and padded hip and thigh panels. The jerseys, too, are padded in the shoulders (for carrying your bike over obstacles) and in the arms and elbows (to protect against brush and falls).

Fabrics range from nylon/Lycra with a heavier weight and tighter weave, than on-road clothing, to nearly snagproof, thick-thread, Cordura nylon. Kevlar, a strong and abrasion-resistant fiber used in bulletproof vests, has been woven into ATB shorts. Entrant, a breatheable/waterproof fabric, is included in some shorts panels, as are Swisstex, polypropylene/Lycra, and cotton blends. Some fabrics are even being chemically treated to repel mud, grease, and water. And if you're confused by such high-tech terminology, take heart in the fact you'll also find good old corduroy in cool-weather ATB gear.

Photograph 2-6. Now great style plus durability help mountain-bike clothing make the grade.

Off-road clothing has, indeed, come a long way when you consider many of today's garments feature niceties such as zippered pockets to keep your keys and loose change secure, mesh panels for added ventilation, and a rugged, more casual look. Accessories include elastic elbow and knee pads, shin guards, and special gloves and shoes. And don't forget a helmet, available now in a variety of colors as well as in the camouflage pattern. Look for a tag indicating that the helmet has met American National Standards Institute (ANSI) or Snell test specifications. Now you can venture off-road wearing clothes as well suited to the dirt as your bicycle.

Maintaining Your Machine – What to Do so the Dirt Won't Hurt

After paying all that cash for a beautiful, new, smooth-running mountain bike, you may be reluctant to head for the mud pits and dusty trails. Don't be. Although Mother Earth can make your 5-hour-old ATB look as if it's suddenly suffered 5 years of deterioration, the dirt won't hurt as long as you take the necessary precautions.

The following tips represent years of experience riding and maintaining off-road bikes by our muck-raking, dust-busting duo, Don Cuerdon and Gary Fisher. Cuerdon's the muck expert, having developed his ATB skills in the lush and muddy Northeast. Fisher, owner of Fisher MountainBikes, helped pioneer off-road cycling on the arid, dusty roads of Marin County's Mount Tamalpais in California. Together, they've seen (and cleaned) it all.

What follows are their best tricks to help you keep your all-terrain bike working well and avoid premature parts replacement. Much of this maintenance can be done in just a few minutes.

Cleaning

The most important rule in ATB maintenance is to de-dirt the bike frequently. Dirt acts as a grinding compound when it gets between moving parts, so the sooner you remove it, the better. In muddy or sandy conditions you may have to clean the bike after every ride.

If you're careful, you can use a car wash. Just don't let the high-pressure wand blast water into the bearings. Almost all ATBs have sealed bearings in the hubs and crank, but no seals are impermeable. And while we're on the subject, never ride with the crank completely submerged. The flexing from pedaling will let water through the seals. Splashing through a creek is fine; riding downstream with a snorkel isn't.

The European method of bike washing works best. You'll need a bucket of hot water, a mild detergent such as Bike Wash, three nylon-bristled brushes, a high-viscosity degreaser such as Gunk, a small screwdriver, a rinse bucket or garden hose, and an old towel. Use a floor brush for the big parts of the bike, a bottle brush for the nooks and crannies, and another bottle brush designated for greasy parts. Now move the BMW out of the driveway and let's get to work.

1. Initial rinse. Remove the major muck by gently spraying with the garden hose or dousing the bike with a bucketful of water. Never wipe dirt or mud from your bike with a rag – it will scratch the finish.

2. Degrease. Remove the wheels. Brush degreaser onto the derailleurs, chain, and chainrings. Mush it between the free-wheel cogs. You must use a high-viscosity degreaser so it doesn't run inside sealed bearings. The thick stuff also removes surface grime from the chain without washing anything into the pins and rollers (which could cause more wear than leaving the chain dirty). Avoid aerosol degreasers – they're too light.

3. Rinse. Use water and the greasy brush to rinse the chain, derailleurs, and chainrings. A small screwdriver is handy for picking loosened crud out of the freewheel.

4. Wheels. Start with the hub, using the clean bottle brush and a bucket of soapy water. Continue cleaning outward until you reach the rim. Scrub the rim and tire with the floor brush. Rinse.

5. Frame. Use the floor brush, then the clean bottle brush to get behind the chainrings and other hard-to-reach spots. Don't forget under the saddle. Rinse and then install the wheels.

6. Dry. Wipe off water with a towel, then put the bike in a warm place to dry thoroughly. The tubes of better ATBs have drain holes to let moisture out and dry air in.

Inspection

It's easier to inspect for damage and other problems when a bike is clean. Here's the checklist:

1. Frame. Soon after you buy your ATB, measure its wheelbase (distance from the rear axle to the front axle when the front wheel is straight ahead). Remeasure each time you inspect the bike. If the wheelbase grows or shrinks, something's damaged. Also look for cracks in lugs or frame joints. These may appear as paint cracks. Inspect tubes for bulges, dents or ripples. If something looks suspicious, see a professional.

2. Wheels. Spin the wheels. Watch between the brake pads for dents, bulges, wobbles, etc., in the rims. Look for loose or broken spokes. Check the tires for cuts, bulges and embedded debris. When the wheels are removed for washing, turn the axles with your fingers. Any roughness indicates the need for cone adjustment or repacking. Look for broken or bent freewheel teeth.

3. Handlebar grips. Twist them. If they move, remove them and apply rubber cement. Use enough so they slip on easily. You'll need a stickier glue such as 3M Fast Tack Trim Adhesive for soft foam grips.

4. Chain. Count 24 links and measure from the first pin to the last. A new chain should measure 12 inches. If yours is 12⅛ inches or more, replace it. Riding with a worn chain accelerates wear to chainrings and freewheel cogs. It also impairs shifting performance.

5. Derailleur alignment. This is especially critical with an indexed system. Sight from behind the bike: the pulleys should be aligned vertically and parallel to the plane of the chainrings and freewheel. Anything crooked should be straightened by your dealer.

6. Brakes. Inspect pads for wear and embedded debris. Check for frayed cables. Replace anything that is even remotely suspect. You must have reliable brakes in the outback.

7. Pedals. Occasionally remove them from the cranks and turn the axles with your fingers, feeling for roughness or excessive play. Then look closely for fractures in the pedal body and cage. Ditto for the toe clips, if you use them. Make sure their bolts are tight.

8. Bottom bracket. With the pedals off, drape the chain around the bottom bracket shell so it doesn't touch the chainrings. Place your ear against the saddle and turn the cranks. Anything funny going on inside the bottom bracket will be amplified through the frame and become audible at the saddle. If you're not sure you like what you hear, remove the cranks and turn the axle with your fingers to check adjustment.

9. Headset. Grasp the top tube behind the head tube, lift the front wheel a few inches, and nudge the handlebar so it turns gently from side to side. If it wants to catch in the straight-ahead position, the headset is damaged. If it locks as if it has auto pilot, it's ruined. The best solution for this is prevention – frequent checks to make sure the headset is properly adjusted. A loose one will clunk when you squeeze the front brake hard and rock the bike back and forth. A tight one won't let the front end pivot fully when you pick it up and nudge the handlebar. One way to get more miles from a damaged headset is to install loose ball bearings in place of the retainers. Additional bearings will fit in each race, so they won't sit in the dents that are causing the catch. You can also have the shop partially rotate the headset cups.

Lubrication

When your bike is dry, lubricate the parts you degreased and any others that may need it.

1. Chain, derailleur pulleys, roller-cam brakes. The lubricant must correspond to the environment. In dry weather, use a product with a volatile carrier that penetrates well, then evaporates, leaving a viscous lubricant in place. Tri-Flow and Sta-Lube are good choices. Use a rag to protect the rear rim from overspray, and wipe away excess lubrication. Lube exposed moving parts of a roller-cam brake.

For wet weather or muddy terrain, a sticky oil works best. Try Campagnolo or Phil Wood. Although they collect dirt, they prevent anything raunchy from seeping into the chain's pins and rollers and the derailleur's pulley bushings. European cyclocross racers sometimes coat their chains with grease when the course is extra muddy. The grease simply displaces the mud.

Paraffin isn't a good choice for ATB chains. It doesn't last long enough, so the chain has to be removed and rewaxed too often.

2. Seatpost. If you use your bike correctly, you'll frequently change your seat height. Lowering the saddle is necessary for good control on descents, so the seatpost/seat tube must be kept clean and lubricated. Remember to mark the post before you pull it from the frame in order to retain your correct saddle height. If you use a Hite-Rite seat locator, put a piece of masking tape just above the Hite-Rite sleeve. Loosen the sleeve and pull the post from the frame. Wrap a rag around a screwdriver and clean the seat tube. Lubricate the seatpost with your "Campy" or Phil oil and reassemble the Hite-Rite.

3. Cables. Free-sliding derailleur cables are always desirable, and they're mandatory with indexed shifting. Grease gets too dirty and creates drag in the system. Shimano recommends running its derailleur cables dry. If that doesn't suit you, try pure silicone spray. Braking performance can be improved by lubricating the cable end buttons at the levers.

4. Sealed bearings. Sealed bearings can and should be serviced. Carefully remove the seal with an X-Acto knife or similar tool. Be careful not to dent the seal's seat. Thorough cleaning of the internal parts is crucial because new grease will be degraded by the old. Use a solvent such as kerosene or a degreaser and water. Wear safety goggles. Avoid getting solvent on the tires or any other rubber parts. Flush thoroughly and dry with compressed air (available by the can at photography stores).

Repack the bearings with high-viscosity grease. Fisher MountainBikes come packed with Sta-Lube Boat Trailer Wheel Bearing Grease. Gary likes it so much he supplies it to the factory in Japan. It's a bit too gooey for road use, however. A better choice for skinny-tire bikes is Campagnolo 10-N, a higher viscosity version of Campy's famous white grease. It comes in a tube instead of a jar.

5. Saddle. Water and dirt can turn your saddle's supple leather covering into something akin to sandpaper. Preserve the leather by rubbing in Brooks Proofhide or Nivea skin cream. Dust the surface with baby powder or talc to make it slippery again.

6. Pump. Avoid pump failures by keeping the gasket lubed. Use petroleum jelly on leather gaskets and K-Y jelly on rubber ones.

Finally, remember you have to get your ATB filthy in order to take care of it right. Happy (muddy and dusty) trails!

Part Three
Off-Road Riding Skills and Street Smarts

Get Good –
Then You Can Get Gonzo

"There's a real quick learning curve in mountain bike riding
... it's either do or die!" laughs off-road enthusiast Hannah North.

Like any other activity, there is a right way and a wrong way
to ride in the rough. Although she doesn't mean for you to take
the remark literally, she makes a good point. If you don't catch on
fairly fast, you could have a few extra knocks to show for it.

Riding an all-terrain bike is not hard, just different. If this is
the year you've added a fat-tire machine to your stable,
congratulations. You're discovering a great new world of cycling,
but getting good on an ATB can be a tad bewildering.

It needn't be. Experienced riders are usually willing to share
helpful tips, and we asked three of the best: San Diego's Hannah
North, formerly a national-class road racer; ATB-builder Chris
Chance of Somerville, Massachusetts; and off-road pioneer Gary
Fisher of San Anselmo, California. Their advice for beginners and
more experienced riders follows.

Practice shifting. This might sound silly if you can operate
a 12-speed gear system in your sleep, but those ATB thumbshifters
aren't at all like the gear levers on a road bike. You have three
chainwheels to deal with, and there are huge jumps between
freewheel cogs. Get used to these things by taking at least one
ride on a smooth road so you can watch the ATB work. This will
pay immediate dividends on the trail, where looking down may
provide just the moment it takes to debark a tree. Save the
trees – learn to operate your ATB's gear system as certainly as
you do your road bike's.

Photograph 3-1. If you know more-experienced off-roadies who are willing to keep a moderate pace and ride relatively easy terrain, you can learn a lot by joining them.

Orient yourself. Before heading to the forest, put some thought into how the ATB sits under you. Develop a sense for the long wheel base, how your weight is distributed, and the steering geometry. Put a stick on the road and ride over it a few times. Learn where the thump comes in relation to your location on the bike. Next, practice lifting the front wheel, then the rear, so you cross the stick without touching it. Get familiar, get comfortable.

Ride alone. Make some off-road forays by yourself so you won't be rushed. Choose terrain that is fun, not demanding. (Later, they'll be one and the same.) A low degree of difficulty now will speed learning and build your confidence. Whenever you run up against something that makes you put a foot down or fall off, don't keep going. Turn around and try it again, and again, until you get through cleanly.

Ride with other people. If you go out with an experienced rider who's willing to keep the pace under control, you'll learn a lot. Watch his or her technique and copy it. It's fun, and you'll find yourself pulling off moves you didn't believe possible. If you falter in a tricky spot, have your friend show you again how to get through. Then do it.

Rethink your saddle height. Road riders lose sleep over correct saddle height, but when it comes to ATBs variety is a virtue. You probably started at the same height you use on your road bike. Experiment – what's right is what feels comfortable and what works on the terrain. Those quick-release seat post binders are not just for looks. A "normal" saddle height with good leg extension works best for climbing, but an extra low saddle greatly improves control and comfort on descents. The Hite-Rite Quick Adjust Seat Locator is recommended by many ATB enthusiasts because it allows changes on the fly.

Consider new pedals. Different pedals can help if your feet slip forward on bumpy terrain. This is a common problem with the rectangular steel pedals on many ATBs. Pedals like SunTour's oval "bear trap" pedals and Shimano's cantilever BMX pedals help eliminate sliding. But be careful – those "bear traps" can do damage (like the real thing) to your shin or calf. Protect yourself with thick knee socks or, in really rough terrain, high-top boots.

Evaluate the brake levers. Will rotating the brake levers slightly put your wrists in a more comfortable position? Many new off-road riders ache from fingertips to shoulders after their first ventures into hilly country. On the long, bumpy downhills fear makes them grip tightly with rigid arms, and then they get hammered by rocks and ruts. If the wrists have to be cocked at an unnatural angle to brake, it's much worse. Good position and relaxation help a lot.

Ponder the handlebars. It's become fashionable to cut down the handlebars, but think twice before you reach for that hacksaw. Small riders usually benefit from narrower bars – they don't have to overextend their arms when making sharp turns at a slow speed. This isn't a concern for bigger riders, who may find that wide bars provide better control. The smart way is to ride a friend's bike with cut-down bars, then make your decision based on function, not fashion.

Become an amateur geologist. Begin working on two dirty skills – analyzing soil conditions and finding traction. There's a never-ending variety of matter under the wheels, and it takes savvy plus concentration to follow the ground that's firmest. For example, it's usually easier to ride in the creek bed than in the soil on either side. When the trail is laced with ruts, make them work for you. Turn where there is a little berm and use it like the banking of a minivelodrome.

Go faster (sometimes). Nobody likes to crash, so it's natural to go slower when the terrain gets nastier. Natural, but often ineffective. No speed, no momentum, no movement. Just a little more juice will often help you, not hurt you. One example is when encountering a washboard surface. More speed may prevent your wheels from banging into every indentation; it will cause the tires to bounce off the tops and reduce the jolts. It's also the fear of going fast that leads to problems on descents. You must not lose control, but it's dangerous to have a death grip on the brake levers all the way down. That will kill your hands and arms. Instead, let the bike roll free on the flatter sections so your muscles can recover, then slow down for the turns and steep drops.

Master the brakes. Braking technique is different on an ATB. Out on the pavement, the front brake stops the bike best

Photograph 3-2. Often the creek bed offers firmer footing than the soil on either side. Just don't go in over the bottom bracket or you'll be badly in need of a lube.

and is relied on most, because the rear brakes could cause the tire to skid. It can happen on an ATB too, of course, but the rear brake is the one to use most often, especially on descents. If the front brake is inadvertently squeezed too hard – it can easily happen when bouncing down a rocky path – you'd better have your helmet on. Many experienced riders don't even put their fingers on the front brake lever when descending. Some ATBs now come with more powerful brakes on the rear than the front.

Check your tire pressure. The recommended inflation range on the sidewall is probably 10 to 15 psi higher than what works best for most off-road conditions. A softer tire gives a broader footprint, which means better traction. It also improves shock absorption. Ride with a full 40 to 45 psi on any descent worth its salt, and it'll feel as if you're hooked to a jackhammer. However, if you're a large, heavy rider, don't go as low as 25 psi on rough terrain. You could hit a hole and bottom out, pinching the tube and ruining the rim.

A little dab will do ya. Many riders pride themselves on being able to go the entire distance without putting a foot down. As you know, trials riding is an event that puts a premium on exactly that. But when worse comes to worst, don't be afraid to use one leg like an outrigger to help yourself stay upright. One move worth practicing before riding steep descents will help you control a skid, make a turn, and slow down – simultaneously. Practicing on a downhill with smooth dirt, lower the saddle and start down, then lock the rear brake and use body English to throw the rear wheel out to the side. Dab with your uphill foot for stability, but keep it on the pedal as much as possible. Once you develop the feel for this, it might get you out of a jam sometime. But do it only when you need to. That carved landscape and dusty cloud might look dramatic, but it's destructive.

Plan for the climbs. When your gear is too high and you have to stand and honk the last few feet, you may not make it. The rear wheel will lose traction, which can happen when sitting in a gear that's too low. Once you know your gear range, it's a matter of eyeballing the particulars of the upward angle and picking the right ratio. When you must stand, you'll do best to keep your weight in the rear. That's yet another contradiction to the road bike and another reason why there's always a challenge on an ATB.

The Mountain Comes to You – Develop Trail Skills at Home

Handling a mountain bike takes more skill than riding a road bike because the challenges of the trail range from ruts, washouts, branches, and rocks to steep, twisting climbs and descents.

As the terrain changes, so must riding technique. You must apply power differently, brake differently, and anticipate new trail conditions. Your moves must become second nature, drawing upon upper-body strength, coordination, agility, and a precise sense of balance.

Surprisingly, one of the best places to develop these skills is your front yard. Lucky thing, too – what better answer could there be for those days when you long to head for the hills and gulleys, but you just can't spare time for the drive. You'll find the following drills are fun, and they develop the talent necessary to perform well on your weekend trips to the trails. Practice them in the order listed for maximum development in minimum time. In case you fall, wear a helmet and protective clothing.

Up and over. To ride over an obstacle such as a log, rock, ledge or rut, you need to lift the front wheel. Practicing on a curb will teach you how to balance the bike, transfer your weight, and apply power.

In a low gear, ride directly toward the curb at a steady, slow speed. When you're within 12 inches, lean forward to compress the front tire while positioning your dominant leg at the beginning of the power stroke (1 o'clock for the right leg). As the wheel begins to rebound, simultaneously pull on the handlebar and push on the pedal. The front wheel will rise and clear the curb. As you feel the rear wheel make contact, lean forward slightly and your momentum will carry it over.

Make these movements smoothly. Beginners tend to yank on the handlebar, not realizing it's the combination of compression and leg power that lifts the wheel.

To ride off a curb or other barrier, hold the cranks horizontal while standing with your weight back to lighten the front wheel. Always keep your front wheel perpendicular to the obstacle.

Jumping. With every fast descent there's the risk of hitting a bump and going airborne, so it's important to learn how to land.

Use the incline where a driveway and curb intersect. Ride toward this spot from the sidewalk at a 30-degree angle, keeping two things in mind: first, stop pedaling before you begin a jump. Stand on the pedals with your weight slightly back, cranks horizontal. Stay relaxed and bend your knees to cushion the landing.

Second, always land on the rear wheel. If you should come down with your weight forward you could lose control or even go over the handlebar.

After you learn to jump, don't practice too often. It's hard on a bike's fork, axles, bearings, and rims.

Steering through obstacles. On a trail, it's impossible to ride a straight line because of rocks and other debris. But if you learn to put objects "between your wheels" instead of riding completely around them, it will improve your bike control and help you maintain momentum on climbs.

To do this, place a can or paper cup on the street. Slowly ride toward it until your front wheel is a few inches away, then steer to the left or right. As soon as the wheel goes past, steer in the opposite direction so the rear wheel can pass on the other side.

One-hand riding. At speed, most steering is done by shifting your weight, not by turning the handlebar. By practicing one-hand riding you'll learn to use your whole body (especially your hips) to turn.

For this drill, choose a safe, flat area such as a yard or cul-de-sac. Ride progressively slower and make increasingly smaller circles, or do figure eights around cans or cups. Alternate hands to develop a bilateral sense of balance.

Wheelies. A wheelie has few practical applications, but it's fun. This trick is an extension of the skills used in riding over a curb. Keep your gear and speed low, compress the front tire, and apply power as you pull the handlebar. Keep your index finger on the rear brake lever and squeeze it to shift your weight forward should the front wheel rise too high.

At first, practice wheelies on a slight incline. This tempers your speed and helps you raise the front wheel. Initially you may have to accelerate to keep the front wheel up, but with practice you'll find a balance point that allows a constant speed as you use the rear brake to counter pedal force.

Stationary balancing. Practice on a sloped driveway. Roll slowly into position perpendicular to the grade. Brake to a stop, turn the front wheel toward the incline, and place the uphill-side pedal just above horizontal. To maintain balance, use pedal pressure to counter gravity's pull. Stay relaxed and don't use the brakes – you can't maintain balance unless the wheels are able to move slightly.

Mastering the Ups and Downs

Newton's Law was never truer than in mountain biking. And those climbs and descents make for much of the excitement – and the challenge – of riding the rough stuff.

When we at *Bicycling* say, "If you can ride a bike, you can ride an ATB," we mean that the bike's inherent stability, convenient controls, and upright riding position make it easy for beginners to master. But not by starting on Repack Road or Pearl Pass. Before you get wild on the hills, you need to develop riding skills that you probably never needed in your paved-road career. Skills such as descending a steep slope without pitching over the handlebar, climbing the same slope without popping wheelies or losing traction, or just shifting smoothly to the appropriate gear before the grade destroys your forward progress.

Shifting and Climbing

Let's start with those exotic low gears. When you need them it's usually right away, as when a pleasant downhill turns tail and runs for the nearest ridge top. But even today's excellent derailleur systems resist gear changes under full load. The trick to downshifting on a climb is to build momentum by pedaling hard for a moment, then ease off just as you shift for the lower gear. With practice, you'll be able to make the change quickly and quietly, then smoothly reapply the power.

As you gain bike-handling skills, your definition of what's rideable will grow to encompass progressively steeper topography. It's traction – not leg strength – that limits off-road climbing ability. To help your drive tire dig in on severe climbs, keep your weight over the rear wheel by sitting far back on the saddle. Also, the saddle height should permit almost complete leg extension, for maximum power. Lowering tire pressure in back helps, too.

Watch out, though, or you'll pop a wheelie with each pedal stroke. To prevent it, lean forward by bending your arms until you find the precise balance point that preserves traction without over-lightening the front wheel. Assuming your legs are up to the task, it's often easier to climb in a slightly higher gear on slopes with loose dirt or gravel. The reduced torque keeps the drive wheel from breaking free and spinning. Experiment and you'll see.

On rocky ascents, keep up your momentum so you'll bounce over small rocks instead of being stopped cold by them. Once you put a foot down on a steep climb, it's tough to push off and get the pedals turning again before you topple over. You might have to hoof it to the next plateau.

Finally, consider using toe clips and straps. They help immensely when climbing. But even when not cinched tight, they keep your feet from bouncing off the pedals, thus saving your calves and shins from the bite of sharp pedal cages.

Getting Down

Climbing takes technique and power. Descending takes tech-nique and guts. As on your road bike, your front brake provides the more powerful stopping action – so powerful, in fact, that it's relatively easy to lock the front wheel and pitch over the handle-bar on a steep descent. Brake the front wheel judiciously and never before positioning your weight as far to the rear as possible.

Small downhills can be taken in stride, but for an extended descent make use of your bike's quick-release seat bolt, sliding the post all the way down to lower your center of gravity. With the saddle out of the way you can squat on the pedals, cranks horizontal, with arms and knees bent to absorb shock. Use your rear end as a counterweight to lighten the front wheel, which helps you lift it over obstacles.

Brake as necessary to moderate your speed, primarily using the rear binder. Never apply the front brake when you're about to hit a rut. You could suffer an instant lockup, a pretzeled fork, and a nose-dive over the bar.

Oddly enough, going too slow on a descent can create handling problems. By creeping down a bumpy hill, your wheels will bounce in and out of every little depression. On a washboard surface, it's smoother to go a little faster, so the tires float along the tops of the bumps. Relax and enjoy the bike's built-in stability. Make steering changes only when you need to avoid something big. Proper tire pressure also helps smooth out the ride. Too high and you feel every rock; too low and you risk flatting from a pinched tube.

Before starting down, shift to the large chainring and a large rear cog. This helps the derailleur keep the chain tight so it doesn't derail over bumps. It also puts your flatland cruising gear only a thumbshift away.

Photograph 3-3. Gary Fisher, one of the originators of the ATB, demonstrates downhill technique: center of gravity back, seatpost lowered, pedals horizontal.

Until you get good at the basics, resist the urge to emulate the most daring rough riders. Remember, spinning wheels provide balance; skidding wheels do not. Save the more demanding descending techniques, such as controlled skids around hairpin turns, for the advanced class.

Putting Yourself on Trials

How is an observed trials course put together – and how can you cook up one of your own? Mike Augspurger, with help from his wife, Leni Fried, designed the trials course in Wendell State Forest described in "More Grace than Gonz – Observed Trials Riding" in Part One of this book. Prior to the event, they spent 4 days scouting locations for the 14 trials sections. Together, they examined rocks, made note of fallen trees, measured the depth of mud holes, and delighted at the discovery of an old stone foundation.

A gifted trials rider himself on motorcycle and bike, Augspurger made sure he was able to master or "clean" each section before including it in the course. Also somewhat of a purist, he took pride in making his creation totally natural. No moving logs or rolling rocks for him. The only modification he will make to a forest is the planting of tiny course markers – red flags on the right, blue flags on the left – to guide riders.

When designing and riding your own trials course, whether it be for a change-of-pace club outing or an afternoon of family entertainment, Augspurger and Fried make these recommendations:

Location. If you have a favorite off-road route, a good place to set up a trials course might be the section where you always have the most difficulty. Simply flag it. Otherwise, look for one challenging obstacle, such as an unusually shaped boulder or a particularly foul mud hole, and build the section around it. In center city areas, you can utilize curbs, trash cans, parking meters, steps, and any other urban flotsam you might find. Include a lot of tight turns if space is at a premium.

Dimensions. Sections are akin to holes on a golf course. Keep them short – lengths of 20 to 30 yards are the norm. To encourage differing strategies, leave at least 2 feet between course markers. If you don't have room or time to flag a great many sections, do as many as you can and ride them in both directions. This way, each section will seem like two.

The Natural

1. Break camp!
2. Be careful toeing the timber.
3. Take a hike up the hill.
4. Lumber over the log.
5. Quit the grousing and do it again.
6. Scout a path over the boulders.
7. Excuse me!
8. Blaze a trail through the underbrush.
9. Don't get trapped in the rock pile.
10. Soft, sandy soil can be a bear if you lose momentum.
11. Water hazard!
12. Spruce yourself up and try again.

Illustration 3-1. Create your own trials course. In the woods, take the natural approach.

Variety. Vary types of obstacles, terrain, and level of difficulty among sections. Design the course so every rider, regardless of ability, will score at least one 0.

Running the event. To keep track of accumulated points, have riders carry a trials card. This is nothing more than a piece of paper on which judges can pen section scores. These are turned in and tallied at the end of competition.

When taken together, all the individual sections are called a "loop." Depending on the size of your course and the competing field, you might make two, three, or even five loops mandatory. To prevent backlogs, have the competitors ride the loop in full before beginning again.

Even though the beauty of trials riding is that all riders, regardless of age, sex, body type or level of athletic ability, can compete equally, you might prefer to divide the competition into divisions to have more winners. A recent National Championships had classifications for BMX (20-inch wheels/under age 14), novice (no previous experience), intermediate (trials-type bike/some experience), and advanced/expert (able to clear logs 2 feet in diameter). Prizes, like primes in conventional racing, might be offered to anyone who can clean a particular section.

Equipment. Fortunately, it doesn't take a lot of fancy equipment to ride trials successfully. Although a specially designed trials bike with its towering bottom bracket (13 to 13½ inches) and short wheelbase (39 to 41 inches) offers a decided advantage, any ordinary ballooner will do if you're just out to have fun. Just make sure the granny gears are working well and your tire pressure is low (25 to 30 pounds). And always wear a hardshell helmet. Even though you'll be moving slowly, the terrain can be just as unforgiving.

Riding tips. Economy of motion is the key to good riding form. Thrashing and gear grinding won't put you anywhere but on your face. Each movement, like a step down a dark corridor, should be deliberate and balanced. Keep the following points in mind and there's no reason why you, too, can't be a Baryshnikov on wheels.

When you watch the experts, the first thing you notice is that they rarely sit down. Their seats are as low as possible and their weight is centered over the rear wheel for optimal agility.

Urban Cowboy

1. Saddle up!

2. Mosey on down those front steps.

3. Watch out for that critter on the right.

4. Use the cinder block to get over the wall.

5. Don't get hogtied by those tree roots.

6. Hop along the curb.

7. Giddyup and over that ledge.

8. Don't let a little brick buffalo ya.

9. Dig in yer spurs and clear that high jump bar.

10. Steer clear of that oil spot (cow chip?) in the garage.

11. Now for some real hossin' around.

12. Over that ledge one more time.

13. Ride herd into the back yard for more adventure.

Illustration 3-2. Even in your own front yard, as designers Mike Augspurger and Leni Fried show, there's no limit to the challenges for the urban cowboy.

Most often, they are in a fairly upright position with knees slightly flexed. Speed is more a hindrance than a help in this event. Accomplished trials riders barely turn the cranks as they pick their way through a course.

Although proper form is important, National Trials champion Kevin Norton emphasizes that "half the battle is walking the section." Never ride a course before studying it. Be aware that your front and back tires take different lines. Even if you fall or fail a particular section, don't quit. Ride through and learn so that you'll be more familiar with it on successive tries.

The strategy of trials riding is also important. The natural tendency is to try for a 0 every time, but unless you're incredibly adept that will only result in a number of failures. If your competitors are busy amassing 5s, you might want to play it safe and dab through an entire section, knowing you'll score no higher than 3.

Advanced Off-Road Drills

You've cut your teeth on the easy stuff, and now you're ready to cut loose on more demanding terrain. Practice is still the key to being master of the mountain. Here are a few exercises to have fun with as you hone your technique.

Skid Turns

On a fast descent you may need to turn and reduce speed simultaneously. This is done by intentionally locking the rear brake. To learn the technique, find a flat, smooth, open area. While riding at moderate speed, stand on the pedals (cranks horizontal) with your weight back. Then tightly squeeze the rear brake lever and skid to a stop. Next, try applying pressure on the right pedal, which makes the rear wheel slide to the right (that is, the bike steers to the left). Then try it in the opposite direction, applying pressure to the left pedal.

If you're careful, you can also experience the danger of locking the front brake. Ride slowly, balance your weight on the pedals, and firmly squeeze the lever. You'll see that it's nearly impossible to keep the bike upright while the front wheel is skidding. Before long, you'll learn how much pressure can be applied to the front brake before it locks and you lose control.

Ruts

Cross a rut as you would a set of railroad tracks – with wheels perpendicular to it. If the rut isn't too deep, try riding in it. This teaches relaxation as it accustoms you to nonuniform surfaces – ruts often contain sand and gravel.

Photograph 3-4. Look before you leap. Never go over a drop-off without first checking out the terrain below.

In shallow ruts maintain enough speed to avoid bogging down. Let the bike steer itself. If the rut becomes too deep or narrow, shift your weight to the rear wheel and gradually stop.

Drop-Offs

Never go over a drop-off without knowing what's below. If you're uncertain, stop at the edge and look.

If you decide to proceed, you must maintain some speed or you could go over the handlebar. Roll to the edge, tap the brakes if necessary, and descend with the front wheel perpendicular to the face of the drop-off. Simultaneously slide back off the rear of the saddle and position your cranks horizontally. This allows the front wheel to touch down lightly, after which you can shift your weight slightly forward and roll to the bottom.

The steeper the drop-off, the more skill it requires. For example, if the face is vertical, you may need to lift the front wheel slightly rather than roll directly over the edge. Beginners should avoid drop-offs more than 1 foot high and heed this rule: when in doubt, dismount and walk.

Taking Your Knobbies to Town . . . Safely

Because, in actuality, most bombers are ridden on-road rather than used for bushwacking cross-country, it's likely you've already taken your mountain bike to town – either as a regular bicycle commuting vehicle or for Saturday morning errands. You may be one of many who've opted for a city bike specifically for this purpose, or you've simply found that an ATB's wide track tires and upright seating seem made for piloting through pot-holes and giving you a good view of what's going on around you. If so, you might benefit from sharpening up your in-traffic technique with a few pointers.

On the other hand, you may be hesitating because you feel uncomfortable riding in traffic. You don't like having a bus do heavy breathing over your left shoulder, so up till now you've kept to the trails and bike paths. If that's so, let's pause to observe that riding safely in traffic is all in knowing how – it's not so inherently dangerous as you might think. Most accidents result from cyclist error – like riding on the left against traffic or running stop signs. If you know correct riding technique and put it into practice, you can ride with confidence and discover a very practical, additional way to use your fat-tire bike.

So let's do a quick brush-up. We can't hope to be comprehensive here, but the basics we do review should go a long way toward helping you avoid the most common cyclist errors we see on the streets.

Adopt the right attitude. As a cyclist you should be able to think of yourself as a skilled vehicle operator, just as you are when you drive. If you need to hone your basic road skills, spend a few sessions in an empty parking lot practicing such maneuvers as:

- Starting from a dead stop and riding very slowly in a straight line.
- Weaving your way through a line of tin cans; try this slalom maneuver at a variety of speeds.
- Looking behind you (over your left shoulder) while continuing to steer a straight line.
- Shifting smoothly and easily without looking down.

Once you know you have good control of the bike, you'll be free to concentrate on taking your rightful place in traffic.

Be predictable. Ride with the flow of traffic by behaving as predictably as possible. Use hand signals – the same ones you once learned in Driver's Ed – and your position on the road to inform motorists of your intentions. Don't weave in and out among parked cars. Rather, ride a fairly straight, predictable (there's that word again) line on the road, and leave enough space between yourself and parked cars so that a door can't be opened in your path.

Think and act like a vehicle. In fact, bicycles are considered vehicles by law. Obey one-way signs and traffic signals, and ride with the flow of traffic. Normally speaking, that means you'll ride on the right side of the road, *not* on the left like a pedestrian facing oncoming traffic.

But as noted above, that doesn't mean you always hug the curb. In fact, you want to be far enough from the curb so that you can be seen by motorists entering from a side street, and to avoid the glass and other debris that car tires sweep onto the shoulder of the road. So whenever the road has intersections, parked cars, cross traffic, or other such variables, ride a little to the left of the right-most path you could possibly follow. You'll be sharing the lane with overtaking motorists. Obviously you'll be closer to the cars passing you than if you hugged the curb, but you'll be more visible. You are entitled to share the road. But "share" is the key word: avoid blocking traffic. If you use your bike like a vehicle, you'll find drivers around you cooperative, perhaps amazingly so.

Be aware. Scan side streets and driveways for drivers who forgot to scan for you. Scan ahead for hazards in your path, and ride only as fast as will allow you to stop or veer around such things as broken glass or craterlike potholes. Be aware of traffic patterns ahead and behind you.

Make sure with a backward look. Before veering around an obstruction or making a left turn, look over your shoulder to be sure the coast is clear. Before changing lanes to either direction, give an unmistakeable hand signal and make eye contact if you can with the approaching motorist. Don't make your move until you're certain you'll be given right-of-way.

Learn left turn technique. There are two acceptable ways of making a left-hand turn with a bicycle . . . and lots of wrong, dangerous methods you want to avoid.

In most cases a skilled, confident cyclist can turn left like a vehicle. To do so, you must move from the right side of the road where you've been riding, across one or more lanes of traffic, to finally turn from the left side of the turning lane. Here's how:

First look back over your shoulder. Is the lane clear, or is the motorist approaching slowly enough for you to cross in front of him or her safely? If so, signal emphatically by sticking your left arm straight out. Make eye contact, then you can face forward again, put your left hand back on the handlebar and cross the lane. If you have a second lane to cross, repeat the procedure. Once you've reached the left side of the turn lane, obey any traffic signals and indicate your left-turn intentions to oncoming traffic. Again, establishing eye contact is helpful. Usually drivers in the oncoming lanes will wait for you to turn but, if not, continue to give a clear left turn signal and wait until the coast is clear.

If, however, traffic is too fast or dense to merge left safely, turn left like a pedestrian. Stay right and ride through the intersection to the far curb and get off the bike. Then when you have the green light, walk the bike across the street. Once across, you can mount up and go on your way.

Pick routes carefully. Some roads in your community may be better suited for cycling than others. So use your judgment. If a road seems too narrow or heavily traveled, perhaps it is. Look for an alternate route.

Light up at night. If you must ride at night (when the majority of drunk-driver accidents occur), give yourself the best protection possible by using real lights on the bike, pedal reflectors (their motion identifies your vehicle as a bicycle), and plenty of reflective tape on clothing and helmet.

Wear your helmet. Wearing a hardshell helmet is always a good idea, whether you are going across town, just around the block, or into the woods. Surprisingly perhaps, many bicycle accidents result from one cyclist's crashing into another. And spills can result as easily from a moment's distraction when you're riding slowly (and have little momentum to help keep you upright) as they can from a brush with a car. So don't save your helmet just for those times when you're riding fast or in heavy traffic – wear it always. One additional bonus: you may find you get more respect from motorists if you do.

Let It Snow –
With Fat Tires You Can
Thumb Your Nose at Winter

Bicycling needn't be a seasonal activity just because you live closer to Manitoba than to Miami. Cold weather and slippery roads might put a damper on riding your road bike, but with the right bike-handling skills, your fat-tire machine can manage the roads quite well.

Sharing a snow-covered road with traffic sounds like a cyclist's nightmare, but it isn't. When conditions get bad, lots of drivers opt for public transportation or a day off. Those who brave the slippery roads drive more slowly and alertly than they otherwise would. They aren't likely to take chances trying to edge by you when they can barely steer a straight line.

Actually, as you've probably discovered yourself, the skinny tires on your road bike will cut through an inch or two of snow to get a bite on the asphalt. But, to ride through deeper fresh snow, or on roads packed hard by traffic, there's no substitute for an ATB with the widest, knobbiest tires you can get. Run them at the lowest possible air pressure that prevents pinching the inner tubes – about 15 to 20 psi for most 2.125-inch tires. Soft, fat knobbies have incredible traction on snow. They're much less likely than narrow road tires to slip out from under you.

Clutching the handlebar in a white-knuckled death grip is the natural response when the rear wheel starts squirming through snow. But it's the wrong response. With fat, knobby tires, the bike isn't likely to slide out. Try to relax your upper body and allow the bike to seek the best traction. Don't fight the bike, just go with the flow.

If you ride an ATB with a high-rise handlebar, you may find that switching to the flat, straight bar preferred by off-road racers will give you better balance and control on slippery surfaces. Just keep pedaling smoothly – don't brake or accelerate suddenly – and you can plow through snow up to 5 or 6 inches deep for as long as your smoldering quads hold out.

For optimum traction on hills, don't use the ultralow granny gears. They provide too much torque, which is likely to make the rear wheel break free with each pedal stroke.

Another secret is to avoid hard-packed ruts that grab your wheels and keep you from steering a path through soft, unbroken snow where traction is best. Once the snowplows have made a couple of passes and traffic has flattened the high spots, you can ride anywhere on the road, but use caution – hard-packed snow can be as slick as ice.

Be alert for areas where there might be ice hidden by new snow. Metal grates, railroad tracks, and manhole covers also are especially slick when covered with a dusting of snow. If you ride the same roads regularly, you'll know where most of these hazards lie.

Sometimes you'll be caught by surprise on a slippery patch. Don't panic. Stay balanced over the bike, make no sudden movements, and let your momentum carry you past the danger. If you try to turn or swerve, the bike will slide out as soon as your weight is to one side of the wheels, dumping you hard. As long as you have momentum and are directly over the bike, you'll stay upright.

Even when roads are clear, be cautious when riding in below-freezing temperatures. Ice from snowmelt or the dreaded "black ice" – invisible frozen spray thrown on the road by passing cars – could be lurking around the next bend. Be suspicious of shady spots, because ice will linger there long after sunlit sections have melted and dried.

You may feel more comfortable cycling at 32°F than at 15°F, but snow and ice are slipperiest at the freezing point. If you can pack good snowballs, use extra caution. At colder temperatures, the snow is drier and provides better traction, so you can ride more confidently.

Your Winter Bike

Once you have the bike-handling ability to stay upright on slippery winter roads, make sure your mount is up to the task. High on my list of add-ons is a set of fenders, absolutely essential when the road is a sea of slush. They'll stop much of the stuff from drenching your feet, legs, and back.

Your bike also needs protection. The chain is usually the first component to show the ravages of salt- and sand-laden snowmelt, so keep the chain well oiled, adding more lubrication and wiping off the excess after every ride. If you lubricate your chain with paraffin or a heavy oil, it may skip in subfreezing temperatures. To remedy this, clean the chain in a solvent such as kerosene, dry it well, then relubricate with a light oil that won't harden and cause stiff links.

Also vulnerable are the inner workings of the hubs, pedals, and bottom bracket. If your bike doesn't have sealed bearings to keep out the nasties, slide rubber O-rings (available at a plumbing supply store) on the axles of these parts. Roll the O-rings over to cover the openings where the axle emerges.

Protect the headset with sections of black rubber inner tube slipped over the races. The heavier the tube, the better. A tube width of 1⅛ to 1¼ inches is best. Cut two sections from the tube, each about 1½ to 2 inches long. Slip over the upper and lower stacks of the headset; to slip over the lower headset cover, you'll have to remove the fork from the frame. But even with these safeguards, the best insurance is frequent inspection and a good quality grease.

Because even the most skilled snow rider must occasionally put a foot down to regain balance, don't tighten toe straps on slick roads. We prefer wide "bear trap" ATB pedals without straps because they provide a good grip on the heavy hiking boots many cyclists like to wear. Why boots? Ever wear light touring shoes while walking a disabled bike through deep snow? Brrrr!

If you insist on clips and straps, use pedals that provide a good grip on both sides. Then you can flip the pedals over and ride clipless when the going gets tricky.

And if you commute on your bike, a good headlight, reflectors, and a rear strobe are highly recommended, as dawn and dusk come much closer together in winter.

Part Four

Scenic Trails
and Backroad Routes

Mountain Biking the Backcountry – Six Terrific Areas

You're getting the hang of it and you're hooked. You've tamed the local trails, and now it's time to break away for a week or a weekend in backcountry terrain. Wildflower meadows and mountain vistas, cactus lands and hidden canyons, pine woods and farm country await you. So where should you go? Physically, it's possible to ride an all-terrain bike almost anywhere, but look into the legalities before you load up your gear for a week in the backwoods. The Wilderness Act's restriction against "mechanical transport" (including bicycles) has placed about 8.5 million acres of public lands off-limits to mountain bikers, but there are still plenty of great areas left. Check with state, county, and national forest agents for land that is open to you. Other good bets are rural parks and cross-country ski centers. To start you off, here are six of the best areas in the United States which, at this writing, are open to off-roadies.

Southern Appalachian Mountains

Georgia's Chattahoochee National Forest adjoins the Nantahala National Forest in North Carolina. Forest administrators have identified several trails for use by all-terrain (and motorized) bikes. The best routes are through river bottoms and along fire access roads. Hickory, maple, and pine trees shelter more difficult "hike and bike" trails, which include short sections where most must walk their bikes. Avoid the Appalachian Trail, heavily used by hikers. And be aware that bikes are not permitted on state park trails in Georgia.

Best time to tour: all year round; snow above 4,000 feet in winter.

Accommodations: camping, cabins, motels.

For more information write: Chattahoochee National Forest, Gainesville, GA 30501, and Nantahala National Forest, Asheville, NC 28802 (campgrounds, maps); Georgia Department of Natural Resources, Parks and Recreation Division, 270 Washington St., SW #707, Atlanta, GA 30334 (state parks, campgrounds); Nantahala Outdoor Center, U.S. Highway 19 West, Box 41, Bryson City, NC 28713 (riding information, bike rentals.) For information on four National Forests (Pisgah National Forest, Nantahala National Forest, Uwaharrie National Forest, and Croatan National Forest), write: National Forests in North Carolina, P.O. Box 2750, Asheville, NC 28713.

Photograph 4-1. Let your mountain bike live up to its name – take yours on tour in the backcountry.

Vermont

At one time, Vermont had more cows than people. It still has more cows than ATBs, but this is changing, particularly in the Green Mountains. Near Ripton, the Moosalamoo Recreation Area is surrounded by Green Mountain National Forest and township roads. Use a map to orient yourself or stop to ask directions at one of the delightful farms or villages you pass. The Green Mountains are thickly wooded, steep and rocky on a very pleasant scale for dirt-road cycling. Only Vermont's main thoroughfares are paved, and many a road that starts out hardtop eventually turns to dirt.

Several cross-country ski resorts permit mountain bikes and provide trail maps. Always ask permission and you'll usually be welcome. Ski trails connect from one area to another through forest land. Choose smaller, less-used trails such as the Long Trail.

Best time to tour: July through October (May and June are buggy for camping.)

Accommodations: camping, country inns, bed and breakfasts.

For more information write: Green Mountain National Forest, Rutland, VT 05701 (campgrounds, maps); Vermont Atlas and Gazetteer, DeLorme Publishing Co., P.O. Box 289, Freeport, ME 04032 (atlas of detailed maps even showing abandoned roads); Rompcycle, RD 3, Box 830, Bristol, VT 05443 (repairs and ATB rentals).

The North Woods, Wisconsin

The same ski trails that attract nordic skiers to northern Wisconsin make great ATB routes in the skiers' off-season. The rolling woodlands of the Northern Highlands American Legion State Forest, north of Rhinelander, are interlaced with trails and logging roads. Grades are mild, with climbs rarely longer than a quarter mile. Touring is best in the spring and fall when mosquitoes aren't a problem. Hikers are rare here and in the Chequamegon National Forest just to the west, where the Chequamegon Fat Tire Festival is held each September. A compass helps distinguish between this a'way and that when trails and roads wander at will. Between Hayward and Cable, ride the American Birkebeiner Trail, site of marathon ski races.

Best time to tour: March through May, September through October.

Accommodations: camping, motels.

For more information write: Wisconsin Department of Natural Resources, Bureau of Forestry, Box 7921, Madison, WI 53707 (state forest and campground information, maps); Chequamegon National Forest, Park Falls, WI 54552 (national forest and campground information, maps); Mel's Trading Post, 105 South Down St., Rhinelander, WI 54501 (bike shop; state forest and area riding information).

Glacier Country, Montana

The North Fork of the Flathead River forms the western boundary of Glacier National Park. Long, U-shaped valleys enter from the east and west, scooped out thousands of years ago by glaciers. The North Fork Road from Columbia Falls gives access to these magnificent green valleys. Most of the riding is on packed gravel roads. The Hornet Mountain lookout tower and Red Meadow Lake campground are favorite destinations. Grades are moderate with mile-long climbs and descents.

Within the national park, Bowman and Kintla Lakes are accessible by gravel roads from a park road along the river's east side. (Bicycles are prohibited on park trails, but not roads.) It's a remote area; services are limited to a small grocery, a restaurant, and a hostel in Polebridge. Glacier is bear country; ask about possible closed areas, and observe all recommended precautions. Dangle "bear bells" from handlebars to avoid surprises.

Best time to tour: July through October.

Accommodations: camping, hostel, motels in Columbia Falls.

For more information write: North Fork Hostel, Box 1, Polebridge, MT 59928 (lodging, trail information); Flathead National Forest, Kalispell, MT 59901 (maps, campgrounds); Glacier Cyclery, 336 2d St., Whitefish, MT 59937 (riding information, ATB rentals).

Colorado Rockies

Colorado's mountains are riddled with unpaved roads that served the now-inactive mining industry. Despite the short riding season and high altitude, this is ATB heaven. The place to start is eight-block-long Crested Butte, a town full of like-minded souls (about 85 percent own mountain bikes). From this town you can ride gravel roads that thread through three major wilderness areas, and there's plenty of after-the-ride conviviality. Single-track trails loop along open sagebrush and aspen-lined valleys, ford sparkling streams, and ascend to rock-rimmed basins like Oh-Be-Joyful. The Pear Pass jeep road connects to Aspen, rising to 12,700 feet along the way. Crested Butte, at 8,800 feet, is a mining town rejuvenated by skiing and tourism. Strict zoning laws limit development and maintain a rustic image. From town, you can day-ride for weeks without using the same route twice, and numerous multiday loops are available. Local riders and bicycle shops will provide directions. The altitude will slow you down, so take it easy for a few days before considering tougher rides through Pearl or Gunsite passes.

Best time to tour: July through September; weather extremes (including snow) possible anytime.

Accommodations: camping, motels, condominium rentals, hot tubs.

For more information write: Gunnison National Forest, Delta, CO 81416; Bicycles, Etc., Box 813, Crested Butte, CO 81224.

Anza-Borrego Desert

It's a great winter escape to Anza-Borrego Desert State Park in eastern San Diego County. This is the largest state park in the continental United States. Basically a broad desert at the eastern foot of rugged mountains, it contains badlands, hidden springs, flowing streams, cactus forests, palm trees, and secreted canyons. Varied terrain that covers more than 600 miles of unpaved roads and a policy that encourages ATB use (though bikes are prohibited on hiking trails) combine to make it a great place to ride when much of the country is socked in by winter. Road surfaces include ankle-deep water, rock, sand, and grassy meadows.

Only the main campground has drinking water. The best bet is to base camp there or from a well-stocked vehicle in one of the myriad of undeveloped sites. Beware of flash floods in Fish Creek Canyon and in Coyote Canyon when there are rainstorms in the mountains.

Best time to tour: November through early April.

Accommodations: primitive camping, some developed camping, and motels in Borrego Springs.

For more information write: Anza-Borrego Desert State Park, P.O. Box 428, Borrego Springs, CA 92004 (maps, camping, guidebooks).

Off-Road Vacations the Easy Way – Organized Group Tours

If you'd welcome some professional organization for your fat-tire holiday and perhaps a touch of luxury, try an organized tour. The following list will get you started. (Inclusion in the list is not meant as an endorsement, however, and the types of accommodations will vary. Follow up with your own inquiry to be sure a group meets your requirements.)

Organized Group Tours

American Wilderness Experience
P.O. Box 1486
Boulder, CO 80306
Phone: (303) 444-2632
Tours in Peru

Arrow to the Sun
P.O. Box 115
Taylorsville, CA 95983
Phone: (916) 284-6263
Tours in California

Baha Expeditions
2625 Garnet Ave.
San Diego, CA 92109
Phone: (619) 581-3311 or
(800) 843-6967
Tours in Baja, Mexico

Bikecentennial
P.O. Box 8308-A8
Missoula, MT 59807
Phone: (406) 721-1776
Tours in Montana

Blue Ridge Biking
P.O. Box 504
Montezuma, NC 28653
Phone: (704) 733-5566
Tours in North Carolina,
Tennessee, Virginia

Boojum Expeditions
2625 Garnet Ave.
San Diego, CA 92109
Phone: (619) 581-3301 or
(800) 843-6967
Tours in China, Tibet

Cycle Tours
2007 39th St.
Des Moines, IA 50310
Phone: (515) 255-5352
Travel agency for tours to many
destinations, including: California, Hawaii, Utah, Vermont,
Virginia, Baja (Mexico), China,
Papua New Guinea, and more

Desert Wind Excursions
102 West San Francisco St.,
  Suite 16
Santa Fe, NM 87501
Phone: (505) 982-5329
Tours in Arizona, California, New
  Mexico

Engle Expeditions
2507 Eide St., Suite #5
Anchorage, AK 99669
Phone: (907) 277-1111
Tours in Alaska, Japan

Epic Educational Expeditions
P.O. Box 209
Sun Valley, ID 83353
Phone: (208) 788-4995
Tour in conjunction with medi-
  cal seminar; destination
  varies each year

Four Seasons Cycling
P.O. Box 203
Williamsburg, VA 23187
Phone: (804) 253-2985
Tours in Virginia, Australia,
  England, Switzerland

Journey Associates
1030 West Southern Ave.
Mesa, AZ 85210
Phone: (602) 833-8384
Tours in Australia, Austria,
  England, France, Germany,
  New Zealand, Switzerland

Maine Coast Cyclers
8 Pepperell Sq.
Saco, ME 04072
Phone: (207) 283-1086 or
  (802) 496-4603 (winter)
Tours in Maine

Michigan Bicycle Touring
3512 Red School Rd. RP
Kingsley, MI 49649
Phone: (616) 236-5885
Tours in Michigan, Canada

Mountain Rambles
R.D. #1, Box 308A
Hughesville, PA 17737
Phone: (717) 584-2806
Tours in Pennsylvania

Nantahala Outdoor Center
U.S. 19W Box 41
Bryson City, NC 28713
Phone: (704) 488-2175
Tours in North Carolina

Off the Deep End Travels
P.O. Box 7511
Jackson, WY 83001
Phone: (800) 223-6833 or
  (307) 733-8707
Tours in Wyoming, Papua New
  Guinea, Tahiti, Fiji

Rim Tours
94 West 1st St.
Moab, UT 84532
Phone: (801) 259-5223
Tours in Utah

Spokesongs
130 Fir St.
St. Paul, MN 55115
Phone: (612) 429-2877
Tours in Minnesota, Wisconsin,
Canada

Vermont Bicycle Touring
Box 711-KA
Bristol, VT 05443
Phone: (802) 453-4811
Tours in Vermont

Vermont Country Cyclers
P.O. Box 145
Waterbury Center, VT 05677
Phone: (802) 244-5215
Tours in Vermont

Victor Vincente of America
1582 Pride St.
Simi Valley, CA 93065
Phone: (805) 527-1991
Tours in California, Philippines

Wilderness Bicycle Tours
P.O. Box 692
Topanga, CA 90290
Phone: (213) 455-2544
Tours in California

Womantrek
1411 East Olive Way
Box 20643
Seattle, WA 98102
Phone: (206) 325-4772
Tours in China, Nova Scotia
(Canada)

Credits

Except as indicated, the information in this book is drawn from these and other articles from *Bicycling* magazine.

"Hit the Dirt — Off-Road Riding Can Make You a Better Cyclist" Fred Matheny, "Go Ahead, Get Dirty," *Bicycling*, May 1987, pp. 76-78.

"More Grace Than Gonz — Observed Trials Riding" Joe Kita, "Trials and Tribulations," *Bicycling*, February 1986, pp. 20-24.

"Fat-Tire Racing — Don't It Make You Want to Shout 'Mama!' " Stuart Stevens, "Don't It Make You Want to Shout 'Mama!'" *Bicycling*, March 1986, pp. 40-44.

"Roadies and Mudders Go Head-to-Head over Fitness" Tim Blumenthal, "Who's Fitter?" *Bicycling*, October 1986, pp. 36-42.

"The ABCs of Buying an ATB" John Kukoda, "Everything You Always Wanted to Know . . . about Buying an ATB but Were Too Confused to Ask," *Bicycling*, May 1987, pp. 80-82.

"The Bikes Have Never Been Better" John Kukoda, "ATB Best Buys," *Bicycling*, May 1987, pp. 84-91.

"Time to Re-Tire?" Nelson Pena, "Get a Grip," *Bicycling,* May 1987, pp. 98-100.

"The Right Stuff for Off-Road" Fred Zahradnik, "Fat Frills," *Bicycling,* May 1987, pp. 94-95; "New Products," *Bicycling,* March 1986, p. 14; "New Products," *Bicycling,* May 1986, p. 23; "New Products," *Bicycling,* July 1986, p. 12.

"Dirty Duds—All-Terrain Clothing Comes of Age" Fred Zahradnik and Liz Fritz, "Dirty Duds," *Bicycling,* May 1987, pp. 115-119.

"Maintaining Your Machine—What to Do so the Dirt Won't Hurt" Don Cuerdon and Gary Fisher, "The Care and Cleaning of an ATB," *Bicycling,* May 1987, pp. 120-127.

"Get Good—Then You Can Get Gonzo" Ed Pavelka, "Tips for Rough Riders," *Bicycling,* August 1985, pp. 88-90.

"The Mountain Comes to You—Develop Trail Skills at Home" John Lehrer, "Homework," *Bicycling,* May 1987, pp. 110-112.

"Mastering the Ups and Downs" John Kukoda, "Off-Road Insights," *Bicycling,* October 1986, pp. 62-65.

"Putting Yourself on Trials" Joe Kita, "Putting Yourself on Trials," *Bicycling,* February 1986, pp. 20-21.

"Advanced Off-Road Drills" John Lehrer, "Advanced Trail Techniques," *Bicycling,* May 1987, p. 112.

"Taking Your Knobbies to Town . . . Safely" Susan Weaver.

"Let It Snow—With Fat Tires You Can Thumb Your Nose at Winter" John Kukoda, "Winter Cycling," *Bicycling,* December 1986, pp. 70-71.

"Mountain Biking the Backcountry—Six Terrific Areas" Stuart E. Crook, "ATB Adventurelands," *Bicycling,* March 1986, pp. 78-85.

"Off-Road Vacations the Easy Way—Organized Group Tours" Susan Weaver and Sheila Miller.

Photos and Illustrations

David Epperson: photos 1-1, 3-2, and 4-2; John P. Hamel: photos 1-3, 1-4, 2-6, and 3-4; Donna Hornberger: photos 2-3 and 2-5; L. William Langdon: photo 1-2; Mitch Mandell: photo 3-3; Sally Shenk Ullman: photo 3-1; Robert Walch: photos 2-1, 2-2, and 2-4; Rodale Press Photography Department: photo 4-1.